OLD TESTAMENT HISTORY

I

FROM THE CREATION TO THE
CROSSING OF THE RED SEA

OLD TESTAMENT HISTORY

SERIES

Each Volume is intended to provide material for one term's work. The following are some of the chief features of the series:

1. The Narrative is given for the most part in the words of the Authorized Version.

2. Brief Historical explanations and general commentary are inserted in their proper place.

3. The chronological order of events has been followed.

4. Each period is illustrated by reference to contemporary literature (e.g., Prophets and Psalms) and monuments.

5. Footnotes are added, but only where difficulties of thought or language seem to demand explanation.

Vol. I – From the Creation to the Crossing of the Red Sea.

Vol. II – From the Crossing of the Red Sea to Ruth.

Vol. III – From the Birth of Samuel to the Death of David.

Vol. IV – From the Accession of Solomon to the Fall of the Northern Kingdom.

Vol. V – From Hezekiah to the End of the Canon.

OLD TESTAMENT HISTORY

FROM THE CREATION TO THE CROSSING OF THE RED SEA

BY THE REV.

J. M. HARDWICH, M.A.

LATE SCHOLAR OF ST. JOHN'S COLLEGE, CAMBRIDGE
AND BELL UNIVERSITY SCHOLAR
ASSISTANT MASTER AT RUGBY SCHOOL

AND THE REV.

H. COSTLEY-WHITE, M.A.

LATE SCHOLAR OF BALLIOL COLLEGE, OXFORD
AND ASSISTANT MASTER AT RUGBY SCHOOL
HEAD MASTER OF BRADFIELD COLLEGE

PERIOD I.

(second impression)

Originally published by
JOHN MURRAY, LONDON, 1913

This edition published by Living Library Press, Bristol TN, USA, © 2023

THE aim of this series may be stated briefly: it is an attempt to combine the advantages of a general history with those of the ordinary commentary. The former is open to the charge that it does not make the reader familiar with the language of the Bible, while the latter is too often overloaded with notes and does not cover sufficient ground.

Practical experience has shown that the Old Testament may conveniently be divided into five periods, each containing enough matter to occupy one school term. Without laying claim to any credit for originality, the editors have tried to keep certain definite aims in view: the chronological sequence of events, the historical setting of the narrative, the use of the words of the Bible wherever possible, and, in the later volumes, illustration from the Prophets and other portions of the Scriptures. Footnotes have been added where it seemed necessary, many of them being merely verbal explanations drawn from the Revised Version.

In the preparation of this volume the first two of the Westminster Commentaries, *Genesis* by Professor Driver, and *Exodus* by Mr. McNeile, have been in constant use, and the first duty of the editors is gratefully to acknowledge their debt to these works. Dr. Hastings'*Dictionary of the Bible* and Mr. Murray's *Illustrated Bible Dictionary*, representing as they do two different schools of thought have been consulted on numberless details.

The modern literature of the subject is large, but much of it is necessarily of a critical and almost controversial nature; so reference here will be made only to Dr. Geikie's *Hours with the Bible*, vol. i., which gives an interesting survey of the greater part of the period.

The attention of the reader is drawn to two points: geographical information is confined for the most part to Index I; and it is most essential to use throughout some good map: *Murray's Handy Classical Maps, Palestine*, etc., contain everything that is required. But, for immediate reference, a sketch-map has been added at the end of the volume; and for the preparation of this the editors are indebted to their pupil, S. F. Gooden.

The student is also urged to avail himself of two commonly neglected things, viz. references (which are few), and the General Index, by means of which the repetition of footnotes is avoided.

Finally, the editors wish to thank Mr. H. H. Symonds for much help and advice, and the Rev. C. Mayne for most kindly reading through the proof-sheets.

CONTENTS

CONTENTS

CONTENTS

APPENDICES

INTRODUCTION

THE BIBLE—The word Bible has an interesting history. The original in Greek (*ta biblia*) is plural, and means "the books"; adopted as a Latin word, Biblia, it was at first plural, but later was treated as singular; and hence it is that the English came to regard "the Bible" as a single book, whereas in reality it is a collection of volumes, a "Divine Library," written by different hands at many different times. For an account of the way in which what is called the Old Testament Canon grew up—that is to say, how the first of the two great divisions of the Bible came to be what it is—the reader is referred to the Appendix on the subject. At present we need only dwell on the fact that the Bible is not a single work, but represents the whole literature of a nation.

Old Testament—The larger half of the Bible is called the Old Testament—a curious and most misleading name, due to mistranslation. The Greek word *diatheke* means (1) will, or testament, (2) covenant. The use of the word in the first sense is found nowhere in the Greek New Testament, except possibly in one passage (Heb. ix. 16 seq.), and even there a consistent and clear sense is obtained only by translating *diatheke* "covenant"; but in the

Latin Version, the Vulgate, *testamentum* was chosen to translate the Greek word in every instance.

We ought undoubtedly to speak of the Old and the New Covenants, for it is important that we should be reminded that the former collection of books contains an account of God's first covenant with His people, while the latter, in Gospels and Epistles, is a record of the New *Covenant*. A covenant is an agreement between two parties or persons, and in Ex. 24:7 seq. we read: "And he [Moses] took the book of the covenant, and read in the audience of the people: and they said, all that the Lord hath spoken will we do, and be obedient. And Moses took the blood, and sprinkled it on the people, and said, Behold the blood of the covenant, which the Lord hath made with you concerning all these words."

Corresponding to, and doing away with, this old agreement, confirmed by the blood of a sacrificed victim, was the New Covenant, confirmed by the sacrifice of Christ upon the cross, 1 and revealing to the world a new idea of the kinship between God and man.

Versions of the Old Testament—1. Hebrew and Aramaic: the original languages.

2. Greek: the Septuagint.

(For 1 and 2 see Appendix I.)

3. Latin: the Vulgate, translated from the Septuagint between A.D. 383 and 405 by Eusebius Hieronymus [Eng. Jerome), at the request of Pope Damasus.

4. English: (a) the Authorized Version (A.V.), A.D. 1611, produced in the reign of James I. as the result of the Hampton Court Conference: (b) the Revised Version (R.V.), A.D. 1885

---

[1] See Heb. ix. 18, 19.

(N.T., 1881; Apocrypha, 1895).

The Pentateuch—The first five books of the Old Testament have been called the Pentateuch [i.e. five books), which for long, but without convincing proof, were supposed to be the work of Moses, and were called, by Jews and Christians alike, "The books of the law of Moses."

Modern scholars who apply the methods of the Higher [i.e. historical) Criticism have added the book of Joshua, and speak of the Hexateuch (i.e., six books), a term by which they imply that these six books were probably edited and revised together as a single volume.

There is little doubt now that, as was the case with many other books of the Old Testament, the Hexateuch was not originally written by one man. Judging from evidence of language, structure, and contents, scholars are for the most part agreed in distinguishing between various sources. The book probably grew up into its present form in something of the following manner. At first stories of the dim past were handed down from generation to generation, together with such songs as the Song of the Sword (Gen. iv. 23). Between 850 and 750 B.C. the "schools of the prophets "produced two collections of these, quite possibly from earlier written sources of which we have no knowledge, one in the Southern and one in the Northern Kingdom. The earlier, or Jehovistic narrative, is so called because in it the name Jehovah (English Versions, "the Lord") is prominent, whereas in the later collection that name is avoided, and Elohim (or "God") is used instead. Each has other very clearly marked characteristics of its own.

In Manasseh's reign, i.e. about 690 B.C., the two were combined into one whole, now known as the Prophetical narrative.

In Josiah's reign, 621 B.C., the "Book of the Law" was found in the Temple: this in all probability had been written in Manasseh's reign, and was identical with Deuteronomy, with the exception of some chapters at the beginning and the end, added later.

Later still, a further and final work was composed, which bears very strongly the impress of a different kind of mind: it was due to the influence of the priests and the entirely altered aspect which the long years of exile had given to Jewish history: this is known as the Priestly narrative, and is marked by the frequent occurrence of formulae and statistics, and by the great importance it attaches to ceremonial law.

The Hexateuch, as we have it, is a combination of these various collections and editions, and dates from the period of Ezra and Nehemiah, or perhaps rather later, towards the end of the fifth century B.C.

For a restatement of the older view of the authorship and composition of the Pentateuch, the reader is referred to Murray's Illustrated Bible Dictionary (1908: art. "The Pentateuch"): and for further detail see also vol. 2 of this series.

Inspiration of the Old Testament—It is impossible to discuss at length this important subject; but it is at least advisable to state the position adopted in this volume. It is briefly this. It has been the Divine purpose to single out a small Eastern people to be the chief, though not the only, instrument for the religious education of the world. This people is the Israelites, who are unique in character, history, and literature, the first two being for the most part seen in and expounded by the third. To the study of this literature we have to bring all that we possess of historical and scientific knowledge, and we must do so fearlessly, on the principle that the truth is great and will prevail. When we do so, we find that in many respects it is similar to the literature of other peoples, and we can trace the records of the nation back into the dim ages when historical fact cannot be distinguished from legend and myth. Starting from a very early period of recorded history we can learn what ideas prevailed then about the times when no records were kept, times when primitive man expressed his beliefs about the great mysteries of existence in the form of simple but beautiful stories, some of which survived and were written down centuries afterwards.

In the Book of Genesis, then, we start with these early notions of the Hebrews, about the origin of the world, about life and death, labor and sin, about the beginning of social and political life, about the origin of the Hebrews themselves. Insensibly as we proceed, we find more and more of true history. From religious truth and teaching, which we see in the first verse, we pass to historical truth, at first sketched in broad outline, but afterwards painted in detail. But from end to end of the Canon, Genesis to Malachi, the dominant characteristic is religious teaching, a progressive revelation leading up to the final revelation in Christ. Consequently, as Christians, we arrive at our belief in the inspiration of the Old Testament. We believe in Christ, who appeared to the Jews, and is in Himself the climax and fulfilment of the Old Testament Scriptures; and these Scriptures are the most important of the means divinely appointed as the preparation of the world for the Gospel. Therefore, we speak of them as "inspired." (For a more detailed statement see vol. 2)

ADDENDUM

Note on The Garden of Eden (Gen. 2:8-14)

An interesting note on this subject comes from Sir W. Willcocks, who is engaged in works of irrigation in Mesopotamia. He identifies Eden as the land west of Bagdad. According to his theory, not only Eden, but all the four rivers, together with the land of Havilah and the land of Cush, can be located fairly accurately: the whole forms a district subject to annual floods, with the exception of a small part of the plain towards Bagdad, where the Arabs of today take refuge with their flocks when the floods are out: this spot Sir William Willcocks considers to be the actual Garden, the scene of the story of Adam and Eve and the Fall.

It may be noticed that in Gen. ii. 6 ("there went up a mist from the earth, and watered the whole face of the ground") some scholars prefer to translate "flood" instead of "mist," an interpretation which increases the probability of a theory already sufficiently attractive.

PART I

THE ORIGIN OF LIFE AND CIVILIZATION

GENESIS

*N*AME and contents—The name of the first book of the Bible is a Greek word taken from the Septuagint, or Greek version, and means "origin " (genesis).

A short analysis of the contents of Genesis will show most clearly how suitable the name is:

(1) PRIMEVAL: **Genesis 1-11**—These narratives give us the primitive notions of the Hebrews about the beginnings of things—life and death, the universe and the earth, sin and labor, the making of music and the diversity of languages, and so forth.

(2) PATRIARCHAL: **Genesis 12-50**—In the lives of the Patriarchs, from Abraham to Joseph, we have the origin of the Hebrew nation, ending with the migration of the family of Jacob to Egypt.

Genesis and modern science—The whole teaching of modern science combines to prove the immense age of the planet on which we live, and the great, though lesser, antiquity of the race of man. The three sciences which bear directly on this subject are astronomy, geology, and ethnology. "A recent work on astronomy places the time at which the moon was flung off from the then liquid earth at about 57,000,000 years ago" (Driver). Geologists give us no less than twelve periods, during which the gradual development of life, both animal and vegetable, may be traced, up to the appearance of man. The teaching of ethnology, the science of the growth of nations, shows how infinitely slow is the growth and development of the different types of the human race, with their many and widely scattered branches.

That the history of *civilized* man goes back to an earlier date than would be implied by the chronology of Genesis has been demonstrated by historians and archaeologists, mainly in consequence of the success of recent excavations. Not only can it be stated now "that the existence of man in the Valley of the Nile may be traced back even to the Palaeolithic Period in Egypt," far back, that is, before the dawn of actual Egyptian history, but it is believed that the first Egyptian Dynasty may be dated 4483 B.C., i.e., half-way through the fifth millennium before our era. (Budge, *History of Egypt*) It is without astonishment, therefore, that we hear of terra-cotta "play-things," exhibited in the Louvre in 1905, of which it is stated that they are "identifiable, without the slightest chance of error, as the objects pulled about the streets of the old town (Susa) by the Chaldaean children of 5,000 years ago."[1]

Genesis and religion—We shall be justified, then, in refusing to look for scientific truth in Genesis, and for only as much historical truth as the trained observer expects to find in the earliest literature of any country.

It is not necessary to pronounce a verdict against any character and say "he did not exist," but insensibly, as we advance, we are conscious that we are stepping out of the mists of legend and myth: Abraham and Joseph,

[1] It follows from what has been said that the figures of Archbishop Ussher's chronology (pub. A.D. 1650), often printed in the margin of the A.V. me not to be relied upon as authoritative throughout.

for example, by their well-defined personalities, impress us as being historical characters; while only a few extreme critics dispute the existence of Moses as a single individual.

What none, however, dispute is the great religious value of Genesis. This appeals to us both as students of the history of religion and as seekers ourselves after
religious truth and instruction.

1. *Importance to the student of religions*—Though compiled comparatively late, the sources of Genesis go back very far into antiquity, and we may notice briefly the following points:

(a) The idea, or revelation, of God is progressive: there is a vast difference between the thought of Jehovah as He walked in the Garden of Eden, or the Divine Being who wrestled with Jacob, and the same Jehovah who imposed upon Moses the task of announcing Him to the Israelites in Egypt. The former is spoken of as a glorified man; the language used to describe Him is pre-eminently *anthropomorphic*[1]: the latter is a finer conception of Deity; there is more of the mysterious and the spiritual about Him—[N.B. All language about God, being written by man to suit the understanding of man, must to some extent be anthropomorphic.]

(b) When compared with the religions of other countries the Hebrew religion is seen at once to be, from the start, immeasurably purer. It is not improbable that the story of the Creation in Genesis is to some extent influenced by early Babylonian legend; but whether this is so or not (see below, p. 8), the contrast between the two is complete: the Babylonian myth tells of a crowd of

---

[1]From anthropos and morphe = representing God as possessing the form, or attributes, of man.

deities, themselves produced out of chaos; the Hebrew narrative begins simply, "In the beginning God created the heaven and the earth." In spite of some difficulties, such as the plural word for God (Elohim), the use of the first person plural, and the three men who visited Abraham, the religion of Genesis is clearly monotheistic. Throughout the Old Testament Hebrew religion is, broadly speaking, simple, pure, and moral, entirely free from the degrading elements that are found in the polytheistic religions of other countries.

2. *Moral importance*—The value of Genesis to Christians of today is so obvious as to require little more than the mere statement. At the same time This statement should be emphasized at every stage of the narrative, for as an elementary moral handbook Genesis is unsurpassed. It purposes to represent the thought of the world in its infancy, and both the child and the adult can still profit by its lessons and illustrations, which are unmistakable and striking.

There are many other points of view which combine to make the book perhaps the most fascinating study in all literature, for it appeals to the student of folk-lore and archaeology, to the philosopher and the lover of literature alike. But a complete appreciation of its greatness is only possible after the reader has worked through it in detail with the aid of a good commentary, and has compared with it the primitive beliefs of other peoples.

THE TWO STORIES OF THE CREATION

The division of the Creation narrative into two distinct accounts, of which the former is attributed to the

"Priestly" recension, and the latter to the Jehovistic or earliest collection, is accepted by scholars of both the advanced and the conservative schools.

1. *The Priestly narrative*—Though it is interesting to compare the account of Creation with the conclusions of modern science, it may be repeated that it is quite unnecessary to expect to find, in what is really a prose poem with a religious tendency, accurate scientific knowledge. The probability is that we have here primitive notions, recast and purified at a comparatively late date, intended to teach the people what were regarded as great truths about the origin of the world. It is a matter of indifference whether we regard the six days of Creation as six indefinite periods of time, or as meaning to those who originally told the story six literal days of twenty-four hours each.

Amongst the moral elements of the story may be mentioned the following, (1) It begins with God, who is the Author and Master-mind throughout; He has no rival, and He is from eternity; the creative power is His Spirit, (2) The evidence of the working of the Master-mind is the orderliness of His work, (3) The work itself is progressive, leading up to man: for man is the climax of creation, he is made in God's image, and everything exists for him. (4) Everything created is good, according to the Divine purpose, (5) The Sabbath "rest is a Divinely appointed institution."

When we compare the Babylonian epic of Creation,[1]

---

[1]There is a second and quite distinct Babylonian account of the Creation, which is to be compared with the "Prophetic" Hebrew story in Gen. ii. In both of these the creation of man is placed first, before that of any other form of life.

which is earlier in date, we find some obvious parallels and many still more obvious differences.

The Babylonian version traces everything back to Apsu (ocean) and Tiamat ("mother of them all"). First there was "a time when of the gods none had come forth"; ages later arose a host of gods; civil war began, and Marduk, "the God of light and order," overcomes Tiamat. Marduk then carries out the work of creation. Professor Whitehouse mentions eight points of similarity with the Genesis story; but they have to be looked for, whereas the contrast between the two is apparent. It has been supposed that the Babylonian myth reached Palestine in the middle of the second millennium B.C., and in course of time reached the Israelites, whose religious genius recast it entirely.

2. *The Jehovistic narrative*—The second narrative is the earlier, and has a "prophetic" tendency. God is represented less as a Spirit than as an immortal being such as Zeus was to the Greeks; that is to say, he is described in language which is more suitable to man (see p. 5, note); e.g. iii. 8, "They heard the voice of the Lord God walking in the garden in the cool of the day."

The creation of man is given greater importance, and the cosmogony (i.e., account of the origin of the cosmos, or universe) is shorter than that of the preceding chapter, and cannot be entirely reconciled with it. The other features are the story of the Garden of Eden, the creation of woman, the Fall, and the consequent doom pronounced against Adam and Eve.

Here again, besides the merely intellectual interest aroused in almost every verse, there is a very definite religious value in the story. Even though the Fall may not be an historical fact, yet the account represents vividly great spiritual truths, namely, (i) that man's nature is tainted, contains degrading elements; (2) man is to be purified of these elements (sin); (3) hence labor and the idea of death as the penalty of sin become the means of purification; (4) the final atonement (*at-one-ment*) is the goal of man and the purpose of God. (See Gore's The New Theology and the Old Religion, pp. 76, 77, 233).

THE CREATION: FIRST STORY

Genesis 1:1—2:3

First Day. Light: Day and Night—1. In the beginning God created the heaven and the earth. 2. And the earth was without form, and void; and darkness was upon the face of the deep. And the Spirit of God moved upon

1. According to the narrative, the order of creation was as follows:
1st day—Light (day and night).
2nd day—The "firmament" of heaven, separating the waters below (i.e. the sea) from the waters above (i.e. the rain).
3rd day—Division of continent and ocean; creation of vegetable life.
4th day—Sun, moon, and stars.
5th day—Fish and bird life.
6th day—Beasts and reptiles; man, male and female. Man is given authority. The vegetable world is given for food to man and beast.

1. **God.** Heb. Elohim, a plural word, commonly used with a singular verb.

created. The Hebrew word signifies a Divine act: it is used in Is. 50:25, 26, which is worth quoting (R.V.): "To whom then will ye liken me, that I should be equal to him? saith the Holy One. Lift up your eyes on high, and see who hath created these, that bringeth out their hosts by number: he calleth them all by name; by the greatness of his might, and for that he is strong in power, not one is lacking."

2. **moved.** R.V. marg., "was brooding." Cp. Milton, *Paradise Lost*, I. 19:
> Thou from the first
> Wast present, and, with mighty wings outspread
> Dove-like, sat'st brooding on the vast abyss,
> And mad'st it pregnant.

the face of the waters. 3. And God said, Let there be light: and there was light. 4. And God saw the light, that it was good: and God divided the light from the darkness. 5. And God called the light Day, and the darkness he called Night. And the evening and the morning were the first day.

Second Day: "Heaven."—6. And God said, Let there be a firmament in the midst of the waters, and let it divide the waters from the waters. 7. And God made the firmament, and divided the waters which were under the firmament from the waters which were above the firmament: and it was so. 8. And God called the firmament Heaven. And the evening and the morning were the second day.

Third Day: Earth and vegetable life—9. And God said, Let the waters under the heaven be gathered together unto one place, and let the dry land appear: and it was so. 10. And God called the dry land Earth; and the gathering together of the waters called he Seas: and God saw that it was good. 11. And God said, Let the earth bring forth grass, the herb yielding seed, and the fruit tree yielding fruit after his kind, whose seed is in itself, upon the earth: and it was so. 12. And the earth brought forth grass, and herb yielding seed after his kind, and the tree yielding fruit, whose seed was in itself, after his kind: and God saw that it was good.

5. **day**. To be taken either literally, as a period of twenty-four hours, or poetically, as an indefinite period of time.

6. **Armament**. The earth's atmosphere, which appears to the eye to be limited by the blue sky above, as by a solid vault, was imagined by the writer as an actual vault supporting the water which supplies us with rain; cp. vii. u, "the windows of heaven were opened," when the Flood came.

9. cp. Ps. 54:6-8.

11. **whose seed**, etc. R.V. "wherein is the seed thereof"

13. And the evening and the morning were the third day.

Fourth Day: sun, moon, and stars—14. And God said, Let there be lights in the firmament of the heaven to divide the day from the night; and let them be for signs, and for seasons, and for days, and years: 15. and let them be for lights in the firmament of the heaven to give light upon the earth: and it was so. 16. And God made two great lights; the greater light to rule the day, and the lesser light to rule the night: he made the stars also. 17. And God set them in the firmament of the heaven to give light upon the earth, 18. and to rule over the day and over the night, and to divide the light from the darkness: and God saw that it was good. 19. And the evening and the morning were the fourth day.

Fifth Day: bird and fish life—20. And God said, Let the waters bring forth abundantly the moving creature that hath life, and fowl that may fly above the earth in the open firmament of heaven. 21. And God created great whales, and every living creature that moveth, which the waters brought forth abundantly, after their kind, and every winged fowl after his kind: and God saw that it was good. 22. And God blessed them, saying, Be fruitful, and multiply, and fill the waters in the seas, and let fowl multiply in the earth. 23. And the evening and the morning were the fifth day.

Sixth Day: beasts and reptiles—24. And God said, Let the earth bring forth the living creature after his kind, cattle, and creeping thing, and beast of the earth after his kind: and it was so. 25. And God

21. whales, means sea-monsters of all kinds.

made the beast of the earth after his kind, and cattle after their kind, and every thing that creepeth upon the earth after his kind: and God saw that it was good.

Man, male and female—26. And God said, Let us make man in our image, after our likeness: and let them have dominion over the fish of the sea, and over the fowl of the air, and over the cattle, and over all the earth, and over every creeping thing that creepeth upon the earth. 27. So God created man in his own image, in the image of God created he him; male and female created he them. 28. And God blessed them, and God said unto them, Be fruitful, and multiply, and replenish the earth, and subdue it: and have dominion over the fish of the sea, and over the fowl of the air, and over every living thing that moveth upon the earth. 29. And God said, Behold, I have given you every herb bearing seed, which is upon the face of all the earth, and every tree, in the which is the fruit of a tree yielding seed; to you it shall be for meat. 30. And to every beast of the earth, and to every fowl of the air, and to every thing that creepeth upon the earth, wherein there is life, I have given every green herb for meat: and it was so. 31. And God

26. **Let us make**. There are three theories to account for the plural (cp. 11:7; 3:22; Is. 6:8): (1) it refers to Jehovah and "all the host of heaven "; (2) some see in it an allusion to the doctrine of the Trinity; (3) it is simply the "royal" plural.

in our image, etc. "Both words [image and likeness] refer here evidently to spiritual resemblance alone. ... It can be nothing but the gift of self-conscious reason, which is possessed by man, but by no other animal" (Driver).

29, 30. These verses seem to suppose that man and the animal world were originally vegetarian, whereas palaeontology, the science which deals with fossils, teaches us that before man appeared carnivorous animals existed. See 9:2 seq. and note.

30. **life**. Heb. "a living soul."

saw every thing that he had made, and, behold, it was very good. And the evening and the morning were the sixth day.

Seventh Day: the Sabbath—ii. 1. Thus the heavens and the earth were finished, and all the host of them. 2. And on the seventh day God ended his work which he had made; and he rested on the seventh day from all his work which he had made. 3. And God blessed the seventh day, and sanctified it: because that in it he had rested from all his work which God created and made.

The Creation: Second Story

Genesis 2:4 —3:24

The earth and man—4. These are the generations of the heavens and of the earth when they were created, in the day that the Lord God made the earth and the heavens, 5. and every plant of the field before it was in the earth, and every herb of the field before it grew: for the Lord God had not caused it to rain upon the earth, and there was not a man to till the ground. 6. But there went up a mist from the earth, and watered the whole face of the ground. 7. And the

3. **rested.** The Hebrew word recalls the "Sabbath," which was not instituted till later (Ex. 20:8 seq.).

4. **These are the generations**, a formula which elsewhere comes at the beginning of the passage to which it refers; and so Dr. Driver, who places it at the end of the First Creation story, suggests that either "these" refers back to the work of the Six Days, or the formula has been transposed from the beginning of 1:1.

the LORD. This expression, when printed in capitals, always represents the Hebrew name, Jehovah. (See Introd., p. xiii.)

5. Read with the R.V. (after a full stop): "And no plant of the field was yet in the earth, and no herb of the field had yet sprung up."

Lord God formed man of the dust of the ground, and breathed into his nostrils the breath of life; and man became a living soul.

The Garden of Eden—8. And the Lord God planted a garden eastward in Eden; and there he put the man whom he had formed. 9. And out of the ground made the Lord God to grow every tree that is pleasant to the sight, and good for food; the tree of life also in the midst of the garden, and the tree of knowledge of good and evil. 10. And a river went out of Eden to water the garden; and from thence it was parted, and became into four heads. 11. The name of the first is Pison: that is it which compasseth the whole land of Havilah, where there is gold; 12. and the gold of that land is good; there is bdellium and the onyx stone. 13. And the name of the second river is Gihon: the same is it that compasseth the whole land

7. ground. The Hebrew word here is connected with the form Adam, "man."

a living soul, i.e. a living creature, the idea emphasized being that of life, not spirituality; cp. 1 Cor. 15:45: "So also it is written, 'The first man Adam became a living soul.' The last Adam became a life-giving spirit."

8. **garden eastward in Eden**. Greek, 7 rapddticros, park; English Paradise; Eden, the basin of the Tigris and Euphrates. The description of the site of the garden contains the most primitive notions that the Hebrews possessed of the eastern land from which they had sprung, and, like all early maps of the ancients, combines geographical fact with imagination. Canals for irrigation existed in Babylonia as far back as the time of Hammurabi (c. 2250 B.C.).

10. *The Rivers of the Garden*. Various theories have been invented to explain these. Two of them, viz. Hiddekel (=Tigris) and Euphrates, the rivers which enclose Mesopotamia, we know; but of Pishon (R.V.) "which compasseth Havilah," and Gihon "that compasseth Ethiopia" (R.V. "Cush"), nothing is known. Havilah, "where there is gold," was perhaps part of Arabia. Bdellium is probably a gum, used for medicine and perfumery; and onyx, in the Hebrew, is a word of doubtful meaning, and has been rendered by the names of various precious stones. The garden lay in the midst of the wealth and mystery of the dimly remembered lands eastward of Palestine.

of Ethiopia. 14. And the name of the third river is Hiddekel: that is it which goeth toward the east of Assyria. And the fourth river is Euphrates. 15. And the Lord God took the man, and put him into the garden of Eden to dress it and to keep it. 16. And the Lord God commanded the man, saying, Of every tree of the garden thou mayest freely eat: 17. but of the tree of the knowledge of good and evil, thou shalt not eat of it: for in the day that thou eatest thereof thou shalt surely die.

Man, and his dominion over the animal world—18. And the Lord God said. It is not good that the man should be alone; I will make him an help meet for him. 19. And out of the ground the Lord God formed every beast of the field, and every fowl of the air; and brought them unto Adam to see what he would call them; and whatsoever Adam called every living creature, that was the name thereof. 20. And Adam gave names to all cattle, and to the fowl of the air, and to every beast of the field; but for Adam there was not found an help meet for him.

Woman—21. And the Lord God caused a deep sleep to fall upon Adam, and he slept: and he took one of his ribs, and closed up the flesh instead thereof; 22. And the rib, which the Lord God had taken from man, made he a woman, and brought her unto the man. 23. And Adam said, This is now bone of my bones, and flesh

17. This prohibition points to the necessity, from the beginning, of temptation, a process of testing, whereby man's moral nature is perfected. Though to fall implies sin, and sin degrades, yet the innocence of ignorance does not exalt the soul like the innocence of conscious and faithful obedience. Thus we see that everything we consider evil (e.g. temptation, sin, suffering) was used by the Creator in the working out of His scheme for the education of man.

18. **an help meet for him**, i.e. a helper suited for him: the expression "help-meet," taken from this sentence, is therefore incorrect.

of my flesh; she shall be called Woman, because she was taken out of Man. 24. Therefore shall a man leave his father and his mother, and shall cleave unto his wife: and they shall be one flesh. 25. And they were both naked, the man and his wife, and were not ashamed.

The temptation and the Fall—3:1. Now the serpent was more subtle than any beast of the field which the Lord God had made. And he said unto the woman, Yea, hath God said, Ye shall not eat of every tree of the garden? 2. And the woman said unto the serpent, We may eat of the fruit of the trees of the garden: 3. but of the fruit of the tree which is in the midst of the garden, God hath said, Ye shall not eat of it, neither shall ye touch it, lest ye die. 4. And the serpent said unto the woman, Ye shall not surely die: 5. for God doth know that in the day ye eat thereof, then your eyes shall be opened, and ye shall be as gods, knowing good and evil. 6. And when the woman saw that the tree was good for food, and that it was pleasant to the eyes, and a tree to be desired to make one wise, she took of the fruit thereof, and did eat, and gave also unto her husband with her; and he did eat. 7. And the eyes of them both were opened, and they knew

23. **Woman ... Man**, representing in English the play on words of which the Hebrews were so fond. The Hebrew here is *Isshah* and *Ish*.

1. the serpent, to the primitive mind, was typical of evil and craftiness: not till very late times was the serpent of this story identified with the devil.

It is interesting, in this connection, to recall the Gnostic heresy of the Ophites. They regarded the temptation by the serpent as the act of a beneficent power, who against the will of the Demiurge, an inferior deity, the creator of the world, enlightened man and thus made him capable of intellectual progress.

Yea, etc. Ironical: "has God really said . . .? '*

5. **as gods**, or (R.V.), "as God."

that they were naked; and they sewed fig leaves together, and made themselves aprons. 8. And they heard the voice of the Lord God walking in the garden in the cool of the day: and Adam and his wife hid themselves from the presence of the Lord God amongst the trees of the garden. 9. And the Lord God called unto Adam, and said unto him, "Where art thou?" 10. And he said, "I heard thy voice in the garden, and I was afraid, because I was naked; and I hid myself." 11. And he said, "Who told thee that thou wast naked? Hast thou eaten of the tree, whereof I commanded thee that thou shouldest not eat?" 12. And the man said, "The woman whom thou gavest to be with me, she gave me of the tree, and I did eat." 13. And the Lord God said unto the woman, "What is this that thou hast done?" And the woman said, "The serpent beguiled me, and I did eat."

The sentence—14. And the Lord God said unto the serpent, "Because thou hast done this, thou art cursed above all cattle, and above every beast of the field; upon thy belly shalt thou go, and dust shalt thou eat all the days of thy life: 15. and I will put enmity between thee and the woman, and between thy seed and her seed; it shall bruise thy head, and thou shalt bruise his heel." 16. Unto the woman he said, "I will greatly multiply thy

---

15. This verse has been called the Protevangelium, or First Gospel; and though originally no doubt it expressed no more than perpetual enmity between man and the serpent race, yet in course of time it was natural for the Hebrews to read more into it, and to regard it as a prophecy of the struggle between mankind and the Evil One; and still more naturally did the early Christians see in it the first reference to the redemptive work of Christ. *cp.* Rom. 16:20; "The God of peace shall bruise Satan under your feet shortly."

sorrow and thy conception; in sorrow thou shalt bring forth children; and thy desire shall be to thy husband, and he shall rule over thee. 17. And unto Adam he said, Because thou hast hearkened unto the voice of thy wife, and hast eaten of the tree, of which I commanded thee, saying, Thou shalt not eat of it; cursed is the ground for thy sake; in sorrow shalt thou eat of it all the days of thy life; 18. thorns also and thistles shall it bring forth to thee; and thou shalt eat the herb of the field; 19. in the sweat of thy face shalt thou eat bread, till thou return unto the ground; for out of it wast thou taken: for dust thou art, and unto dust shalt thou return.

20. And Adam called his wife's name Eve; because she was the mother of all living. 21. Unto Adam also and to his wife did the Lord God make coats of skins, and clothed them.

Man driven from Eden—22. And the Lord God said, Behold, the man is become as one of us, to know good and evil; and now, lest he put forth his hand, and take also of the tree of life, and eat, and live for ever: 23. therefore the Lord God sent him forth from the garden of Eden, to till the ground from whence he was taken. 24. So he drove out the man; and he placed at the east of the garden of Eden Cherubims, and a flaming sword

17. Hitherto the fruits of the earth had grown of their own accord for man's use; now agriculture became necessary. For a similar belief amongst Greeks and Romans, *cp.* Hes., *Works and Days*, 117 *seq.*: Ovid, *Met.*, i. 103 *seq.*; Virg., *Georg.*, i. 127 *seq.*

20. **Eve**. Heb. *Havvah*, i.e. Living.

22. **one of us**, i.e. like one of the Heavenly Host, amongst which were the Cherubim.

24. **Cherubims** emblematic figures of the cherubim formed the Mercy seat, or covering to the Ark, in the Holy of Holies. A detailed description is to be found in Ezek. 1:5 *seq.*, where they are represented as men with wings and four heads: the head of a man, a lion, an ox, and an eagle respectively.

which turned every way, to keep the way of the tree of life.

THE STORY OF CAIN AND ABEL

The original object of this story was to explain the development of sin amongst mankind and the origin of homicide, which in this first instance was actual murder.   There are difficulties in the story which do not admit of satisfactory explanation: it may be asked, Why did Jehovah not accept Cain's offering? How was His displeasure shown? What was the sign appointed for Cain? Whom did he marry? The best reply to such questions is to admit that we do not know but we may add that these early stories are only a selection which do not necessarily form a consistent and complete whole, and that in this very case there are signs that the original story has been cut down and edited.

Among the lessons taught are the following: (i) God judges man's motives rather than his acts; the service of the heart is worth more than any ceremonial. (2) It is not the sin of murder that is condemned so much as the sin of jealousy and malice (cf. Sermon on the Mount Matt. v. 21:6). (3) The great doctrine of the Brotherhood of Man, that each man is his brother's keeper, and has his share of responsibility for the conditions of the lives of others. (4) Sin inevitably brings its own punishment. (5) God remonstrates with man before the climax of the sin is reached.

The Story of Cain and Abel

Genesis 4:1-16

Birth of Cain and Abel—4:1 And Adam knew Eve his wife; and she conceived, and bare Cain, and said, I have gotten a man from the Lord. 2. And she again bare his brother Abel. And Abel was a keeper of sheep, but Cain was a tiller of the ground.

The first murder—3. And in process of time it came to pass, that Cain brought of the fruit of the ground an offering unto the Lord. 4. And Abel, he also brought of the firstlings of his flock and of the fat thereof. And the Lord had respect unto Abel and to his offering: 5. but unto Cain and to his offering he had not respect. And Cain was very wroth, and his countenance fell. 6. And the Lord said unto Cain, Why art thou wroth? and why is thy countenance fallen? 7. If thou doest well, shalt thou not be accepted? and if thou doest not well, sin lieth at the door. And unto thee shall be his desire, and thou shalt rule over him. 8. And Cain talked with Abel

1. **gotten**. The name Cain is not connected etymologically with the Hebrew verb used here, but there is a resemblance between the two, and the writer is using the figure of speech called aronomasia, a play on words.

7. R.V. marg.: "If thou doest well, shall it not be lifted up? and if thou doest not well, sin coucheth at the door: and unto thee is its desire, but thou shouldest rule over it"{*i.e.* "if thou doest well, thy countenance will be bright and cheerful: if thou doest wrong, be sure that sin is waiting to spring on thee, eager to make thee its prey; but it is thy duty to overcome sin"). Cain's offering was merely formal; his life was marred by sin, and he was not repentant.

8. And Cain talked with Abel his brother. R.V. marg.: "Heb. said unto. Many ancient authorities have, said unto Abel his brother, Let us go into the field." Bishop Ryle supposes that the writer, in selecting passages from the original narrative, simply omitted Cain's words to his brother, and that the words

his brother: and it came to pass, when they were in the field, that Cain rose up against Abel his brother, and slew him.

The punishment of Cain—9. And the Lord said unto Cain, Where is Abel thy brother? And he said, I know not: am I my brother's keeper? 10. And he said, What hast thou done? the voice of thy brother's blood crieth unto me from the ground. 11. And now art thou cursed from the earth, which hath opened her mouth to receive thy brother's blood from thy hand; 12. when thou tillest the ground, it shall not henceforth yield unto thee her strength; a fugitive and a vagabond shalt thou be in the earth. 13. And Cain said unto the Lord, My punishment is greater than I can bear. 14. Behold, thou hast driven me out this day from the face of the earth; and from thy face shall I be hid; and I shall be a fugitive and a vagabond in the earth; and it shall come to pass, that every one that findeth me shall slay me. 15. And the Lord said unto him, Therefore whosoever slayeth Cain, vengeance shall be taken on him sevenfold. And the Lord set a mark upon Cain, lest any finding him should kill him.

16. And Cain went out from the presence of the Lord, and dwelt in the land of Nod, on the east of Eden.

"Let us go into the field" represent an attempt to repair the omission. See above, on the story of Cain and Abel.

15. **set a mark upon**. R.V. "appointed a sign for . . ." There is nothing to show what this was, but the A.V. "set a mark upon" is incorrect. The sign, so far from being intended as a brand, was to be his protection.

16. **Nod**, *i.e.* Wandering.

Eden. Cain had been in Eden, though his parents had been driven from the Garden.

The Origin of Civilization

Genesis 4:17-26

17. And Cain knew his wife; and she conceived, and bare Enoch: and he budded a city, and called the name of the city, after the name of his son, Enoch. 18. And unto Enoch was born Irad: and Irad begat Mehujael: and Mehujael begat Methusael: and Methusael begat Lamech.

19. And Lamech took unto him two wives: the name of the one was Adah, and the name of the other Zillah. 20 And Adah bare J abal: he was the father of such as dwell in tents, and of such as have cattle. 21. And his brother's name was J ubal: he was the father of all such as handle the harp and organ. 22. And Zillah, she also bare Tubal-cain, an instructer of every artificer in brass and iron: and the sister of Tubal-cain was Naamah.

23. And Lamech said unto his wives,

Adah and Zillah, hear my voice;

Ye wives of Lamech, hearken unto my speech:

For I have slain a man for wounding me,

And a young man for bruising me:

24 If Cain shall be avenged sevenfold,

Truly Lamech seventy and sevenfold.

25. And Adam knew his wife again; and she bare a

17-26. In these verses is narrated the origin of Civilization according to Hebrew tradition: they deal with (i) city life, (2) nomad life, (3) music, (4) the use of metals, (5) the beginning of war, and (6) the origin of religious worship.

19. **two wives**. The first instance, in the Hebrew narrative, of polygamy.

20. **father**, metaphorical.

22. **an instructor of every artificer in**. R.V. "the forger of every cutting instrument of . . ."

23, 24. **Adah**, etc. The Song of the Sword (printed from the R.V.) celebrates the value and power of the newly found weapon of war.

The sword would be a greater protection to Lamech than the "mark" was for Cain. (See verse 15.)

son, and called his name Seth: For God, said she, hath appointed me another seed instead of Abel, whom Cain slew. 26. And to Seth, to him also there was born a son; and he called his name Enos: then began men to call upon the name of the Lord.

FROM ADAM TO NOAH

Genesis 5

The progress of the human race from Adam to Noah—that is, before the Flood—is represented in chap. 5. in the form of a genealogy, which is introduced thus:

1. This is the book of the generations of Adam. In the day that God created man, in the likeness of God made he him; 2. male and female created he them; and blessed them, and called their name Adam, in the day when they were created.

In the genealogy itself we may notice three points:

1. The great length of life attributed to primitive man: Methusaleh is said to have lived for 969 years.

2. Of Enoch 1 a remarkable statement is made, verse 24:

2. **their name Adam**. See, *Light from the East*, by Rev. C. J. Ball, p. 20: "The Sumerian [i.e. pre-Babylonian— Ed.] *Adam* is literally 'side-spouse,' and seems, therefore, to denote all creatures which exist in pairs, or as male and female; so that it may be used of the entire animal creation, both brute and human. The meaning of the Sumerian term thus explains the story of the origin of woman (Gen. 2:21 *seq.*), and accounts for the curious expression 'called their name Adam' (Gen. v. 2)."

1 **Enoch**. All that is told us of Enoch is that he was the son of Jared (see Gen. 4:17 and Driver p. 8o), and that he was "translated" (*cp.* Elijah). According to St. Luke he was one of our Lord's ancestors. The writer of the Epistle to the Hebrews quotes him as an example of faith (Heb. 11:5). In Jude 14 is a quotation from the Book of Enoch, written c. 100 B.C., a work which, though not found in O.T. or Apocrypha, had considerable influence on New Testament writers. No less than four of the titles of our Lord are found in this book applied, for the first time, to the Messiah.

"And Enoch walked with God: and he was not; for God took him."

3. Lamech (verse 29) called his son's name Noah (i.e. Rest), saying, "This same shall comfort us concerning our work and toil of our hands, because of the ground which the Lord hath cursed." Noah was to found a new race.

STORY OF THE FLOOD

The story—Here, again, is to be found a combination of two narratives, Priestly and Prophetic, no longer written consecutively, as is the case of the two Creation stories, but closely interwoven: these two accounts bear the usual characteristics (e.g. in respect of the Name of God, see p. xiii), and differ in important details, such as the numbers of the animals that entered the ark and the duration of the Flood.

Difficulties of the story—The question which every one must face is, Does the story represent an historical fact? The older view is that it does; that is to say, even though there may have been no world-wide deluge, yet there must have been a vast local inundation in which the waters reached a great height and swept away human and animal life over an immense area. (See Murray's *Illustrated Bible Dictionary, s.v.* "Noah") The general opinion of the modern critics is that there was neither a universal flood nor a local flood on such a scale as is described in Genesis, even after allowance is made for natural exaggeration. They hold that the evidence of geology and ethnology alike is totally opposed to such a theory. There is no warrant for believing that so great a mass of water could have been produced during the period in which man and mammals have existed on the earth; or that, once having been produced, it could have disappeared so rapidly, or that life once more could have been so completely and quickly distributed and increased. In other words, the sum of human knowledge tends to show, without the possibility of contradiction, that the progress of life is infinitely slow and gradual, and the existence of the Genesis story and the parallel stories of other peoples is not sufficient to overthrow this conclusion.

Solution—If the modern view is adopted, a solution is to be found in the fact just referred to, that many countries have independently their own Flood-stories. These are common, but not universal; and it is reasonable to suppose that they all arose from the memory of some specially big flood which in each separate locality was attended with great loss of life. The Babylonian Flood-story 1 should be read carefully, chiefly because of the extraordinary parallels it contains to the story of Noah: perhaps the most striking of these are the

description of the ship, the selection of representative animals, and the sending out of the dove and the raven.

Probably the Babylonian version is older than that of Genesis; but the opposite view is stoutly maintained. However this may be—even if the Hebrew story is not in any way the descendant of the Babylonian—we may reasonably conclude that both are descended from a common ancestor, that both reach back to a time when the Semitic people in Mesopotamia were afflicted by an inundation more destructive than the ordinary floods to which their country was liable.

1 See App. II.

Value of the story—As always, the Hebrew narrative is religious in tone. Emphasis is laid upon (i) the curse of sin, which, once committed, rapidly spreads; (2) the salvation which can be found in righteousness alone; (3) God's mercy in giving man another chance (cf. Rom. 6:23: "The wages of sin is death; but the free gift of God is eternal life").

THE STORY OF NOAH AND THE FLOOD

Genesis 6-9

The antediluvian giants—6:1. And it came to pass, when men began to multiply on the face of the earth, and daughters were born unto them, 2. that the sons of God saw the daughters of men that they were fair; and they took them wives of all which they chose. 3. And the Lord said, My spirit shall not always strive with man, for that he also is flesh: yet his days shall be an hundred and twenty years. 4. There were giants in the earth in those days; and also after that, when the sons of God came in unto the daughters of men, and they bare children to them, the same became mighty men which were of old, men of renown.

Cause of the Flood—5. And God saw that the wickedness of man was great in the earth, and that every imagination of the thoughts of his heart was only evil continually. 6. And it repented the Lord that he had made man on

2. **the sons of God.** A much-debated phrase and passage. The obvious interpretation is this: angelic beings took human wives and from the union there sprang a race of giants, an idea common also in Greek mythology.

3. **My spirit**, etc. An obscure passage, of which no satisfactory explanation has been found: perhaps it means, "My spirit shall not abide in man so long: he is a weak creature, and so his span of life shall be shortened."

4. **There were giants**. R.V. "the Nephilim were." cp. Num. 13:33.

the earth, and it grieved him at his heart. 7. And the Lord said, I will destroy man whom I have created from the face of the earth; both man, and beast, and the creeping thing, and the fowls of the air; for it repenteth me that I have made them. 8. But Noah found grace in the eyes of the Lord.

9. These are the generations of Noah: Noah was a just man and perfect in his generations, and Noah walked with God. 10. And Noah begat three sons, Shem, Ham, and Japheth. 11. The earth also was corrupt before God, and the earth was filled with violence. 12. And God looked upon the earth, and, behold, it was corrupt; for all flesh had corrupted his way upon the earth. 13. And God said unto Noah, The end of all flesh is come before me; for the earth is filled with violence through them; and, behold, I will destroy them with the earth.

Instructions to Noah—14. Make thee an ark of gopher wood; rooms shalt thou make in the ark, and shalt pitch it within and without with pitch. 15. And this is the fashion which thou shalt make it of: The length of the ark shall be three hundred cubits, the breadth of it fifty cubits, and the height of it thirty cubits. 16. A window shalt thou make to the ark, and in a cubit shalt thou finish it above; and the door of the ark shalt thou set in the side thereof; with lower, second, and third stories shalt thou make it. 17. And, behold, I, even I, do bring a flood of waters upon the earth, to destroy all flesh,

9. **walked with God**. *Vide* v. 22, 24.

13. **is come before me**: *i.e.* I have determined upon it.

14. **gopher**. An unknown tree.

15. **cubits**, a cubit was about 18 in.

16. **a window**, etc. R.V. "A light shalt thou make to the ark, and to a cubit shalt thou finish it upward." This perhaps means that little windows, 18 in. high, were to be left under the eaves of the roof, between the projecting beams.

wherein is the breath of life, from under heaven; and every thing that is in the earth shall die. 18. But with thee will I establish my covenant; and thou shalt come into the ark, thou, and thy sons, and thy wife, and thy sons' wives with thee. 19. And of every living thing of all flesh, two of every sort shalt thou bring into the ark, to keep them alive with thee; they shall be male and female. 20. Of fowls after their kind, and of cattle after their kind, of every creeping thing of the earth after his kind, two of every sort shall come unto thee, to keep them alive. 21. And take thou unto thee of all food that is eaten, and thou shalt gather it to thee; and it shall be for food for thee, and for them. 22. Thus did Noah; according to all that God commanded him, so did he.

7:1. And the Lord said unto Noah, Come thou and all thy house into the ark; for thee have I seen righteous before me in this generation. 2. Of every clean beast thou shalt take to thee by sevens, the male and his female: and of beasts that are not clean by two, the male and his female. 3. Of fowls also of the air by sevens, the male and the female; to keep seed alive upon the face of all the earth. 4. For yet seven days, and I will cause it to rain upon the earth forty days and forty nights; and every living substance that I have made will I destroy from off the face of the earth. 5. And Noah did according unto all that the Lord commanded him. 6. And Noah was six hundred years old when the flood of waters was upon the earth.

2. **clean**. Here we have a distinction drawn between clean and unclean animals. See Lev. 11.

3. **by sevens**, cp. 6:19, where only one pair is required.

The Flood—7. And Noah went in, and his sons, and his wife, and his sons' wives with him, into the ark, because of the waters of the flood. 8. Of clean beasts, and of beasts that are not clean, and of fowls, and of every thing that creepeth upon the earth, 9. there went in two and two unto Noah into the ark, the male and the female, as God had commanded Noah. 10. And it came to pass after seven days, that the waters of the flood were upon the earth.

11. In the six hundredth year of Noah's life, in the second month, the seventeenth day of the month, the same day were all the fountains of the great deep broken up, and the windows of heaven were opened. 12. And the rain was upon the earth forty days and forty nights. 13. In the selfsame day entered Noah, and Shem, and Ham, and Japheth, the sons of Noah, and Noah's wife, and the three wives of his sons with them, into the ark; 14. they, and every beast after his kind, and all the cattle after their kind, and every creeping thing that creepeth upon the earth after his kind, and every fowl after his kind, every bird of every sort. 15. And they went in unto Noah into the ark, two and two of all flesh, wherein is the breath of life. 16. And they that went in, went in male and female of all flesh, as God had commanded him: and the Lord shut him in. 17. And the flood was forty days upon the earth; and the waters increased, and bare up the ark, and it was lift up above the earth. 18. And the waters prevailed, and were increased greatly upon the earth; and the ark went upon the face of the

11. cp. on 1:6. The waters supposed to lie under the earth, and the waters stored above the firmament, were both let loose upon the earth.

waters. 19. And the waters prevailed exceedingly upon the earth; and all the high hills, that were under the whole heaven, were covered. 20. Fifteen cubits upward did the waters prevail; and the mountains were covered. 21. And all flesh died that moved upon the earth, both of fowl, and of cattle, and of beast, and of every creeping thing that creepeth upon the earth, and every man: 22. all in whose nostrils was the breath of life, of all that was in the dry land, died. 23. And every living substance was destroyed which was upon the face of the ground, both man, and cattle, and the creeping things, and the fowl of the heaven; and they were destroyed from the earth: and Noah only remained alive, and they that were with him in the ark. 24. And the waters prevailed upon the earth an hundred and fifty days.

8:1. And God remembered Noah, and every living thing, and all the cattle that was with him in the ark: and God made a wind to pass over the earth, and the waters assuaged; 2. the fountains also of the deep and the windows of heaven were stopped, and the rain from heaven was restrained; 3. and the waters returned from off the earth continually: and after the end of the hundred and fifty days the waters were abated. 4. And the ark rested in the seventh month, on the seventeenth day of the month, upon the mountains of Ararat. 5. And the waters decreased continually until the tenth month: in the tenth month, on the first day of the month, were the tops of the mountains seen.

6. And it came to pass at the end of forty days, that

20. *i.e.* above the top of the highest mountain, reaching half-way up the side of the ark.

4. **Ararat**. A mountain about 17,000 ft. high, in the north of Armenia, is now called Ararat; but here the name is used of the whole surrounding country.

Noah opened the window of the ark which he had made: 7. and he sent forth a raven, which went forth to and fro, until the waters were dried up from off the earth. 8. Also he sent forth a dove from him, to see if the waters were abated from off the face of the ground; 9. but the dove found no rest for the sole of her foot, and she returned unto him into the ark, for the waters were on the face of the whole earth: then he put forth his hand, and took her, and pulled her in unto him into the ark. 10. And he stayed yet other seven days; and again he sent forth the dove out of the ark; 11. and the dove came in to him in the evening; and, lo, in her mouth was an olive leaf pluckt off: so Noah knew that the waters were abated from off the earth. 12. And he stayed yet other seven days; and sent forth the dove; which returned not again unto him any more.

13. And it came to pass in the six hundredth and first year, in the first month, the first day of the month, the waters were dried up from off the earth: and Noah removed the covering of the ark, and looked, and, behold, the face of the ground was dry. 14. And in the second month, on the seven and twentieth day of the month, was the earth dried.

Jehovah's decrees about the earth and man—15. And God spake unto Noah, saying, 16. Go forth of the ark, thou, and thy wife, and thy sons, and thy sons' wives with thee. 17. Bring forth with thee every living thing that is with thee, of all flesh, both of fowl, and of cattle, and of every creeping thing that creepeth upon the earth; that they may breed abundantly in the earth, and be fruitful, and multiply upon the earth. 18. And Noah

11. pluckt off, *i.e.* fresh.

went forth, and his sons, and his wife, and his sons' wives with him: 19. every beast, every creeping thing, and every fowl, and whatsoever creepeth upon the earth, after their kinds, went forth out of the ark.

20. And Noah builded an altar unto the Lord; and took of every clean beast, and of every clean fowl, and offered burnt offerings on the altar. 21. And the Lord smelled a sweet savour; and the Lord said in his heart. I will not again curse the ground any more for man's sake; for the imagination of man's heart is evil from his youth; neither will I again smite any more every thing living, as I have done. 22. While the earth remaineth, seedtime and harvest, and cold and heat, and summer and winter, and day and night shall not cease.

9:1. And God blessed Noah and his sons, and said unto them, Be fruitful, and multiply, and replenish the earth. 2. And the fear of you and the dread of you shall be upon every beast of the earth, and upon every fowl of the air, upon all that moveth upon the earth, and upon all the fishes of the sea; into your hand are they delivered.

3. Every moving thing that liveth shall be meat for you; even as the green herb have I given you all things. 4. But flesh with the life thereof, which is the blood thereof, shall

21. This verse may be interpreted in two ways: (1) I will not curse the ground any more as a punishment for man's innate sinfulness; or, better, (2) I will not curse it any more, for I recognize man's sinfulness, and I will forbear.

2, 3. See on 1:29, 30. Man, hitherto vegetarian, is now allowed to eat flesh.

4. **life . . . blood**. *cp*. Robertson Smith, *Religion of the Semites*, p. 40: "The unity of the family or clan is viewed as a physical unity, for the blood is the life—an idea familiar to us from the O.T.— and it is the same blood and therefore the same life that is shared by every descendant of the common ancestor." The belief is a fundamental one, on which the whole meaning of the sacrificial system depends.

ye not eat. 5. And surely your blood of your lives will I require; at the hand of every beast will I require it, and at the hand of man; at the hand of every man's brother will I require the life of man. 6. Whoso sheddeth man's blood, by man shall his blood be shed: for in the image of God made he man. 7. And you, be ye fruitful, and multiply; bring forth abundantly in the earth, and multiply therein.

The Covenant and the Rainbow—8. And God spake unto Noah, and to his sons with him, saying, 9. And I, behold, I establish my covenant with you, and with your seed after you; 10. and with every living creature that is with you, of the fowl, of the cattle, and of every beast of the earth with you; from all that go out of the ark, to every beast of the earth. 11. And I will establish my covenant with you; neither shall all flesh be cut off any more by the waters of a flood; neither shall there any more be a flood to destroy the earth. 12. And God said, "This is the token of the covenant which I make between me and you and every living creature that is with you, for perpetual generations: 13. I do set my bow in the cloud, and it shall be for a token of a covenant between me and the earth." 14. "And it shall come to pass, when I bring a cloud over the earth, that the bow shall be seen in the cloud: 15. and I will remember my covenant, which is between me and you and every living creature of all flesh; and the waters shall no more become a flood to destroy all flesh. 16. And the bow shall be in the cloud; and I will look upon it,

5, 6, declare the sanctity of human life, the taking of which by man or beast will be followed by the punishment of the offender.

13. **bow**. Probably the earliest narrator of the story believed this to be the explanation of the rainbow as a physical fact. It teaches us, at any rate, that even in those times men saw the hand of God in the natural world.

that I may remember the everlasting covenant between God and every living creature of all flesh that is upon the earth." 17. And God said unto Noah, This is the token of the covenant, which I have established between me and all flesh that is upon the earth.

Noah: his family, occupation, and death—18. And the sons of Noah, that went forth of the ark, were Shem, and Ham, and Japheth: and Ham is the father of Canaan. 19. These are the three sons of Noah: and of them was the whole earth overspread. 20. And Noah began to be an husbandman, and he planted a vineyard.

28. And Noah lived after the flood three hundred and fifty years. 29. And all the days of Noah were nine hundred and fifty years: and he died.

CHAPTER 10: THE SONS OF NOAH

In ch. 10 the descent of the nations of the world, except those unknown to the writer and those whose origin is explained later, is traced from the three sons of Noah, Shem, Ham, and Japheth. The division cannot be shown to be in any way scientific: according to Prof. Driver, it is mainly geographical. Then, after the multiplication of languages has been accounted for in the

6 . Cush, i.e. the land south of Egypt, or Ethiopia.

Mizraim, i.e. Egypt proper.

8. And Cush begat Nimrod: he began to be a mighty one in the earth, 9. He was a mighty hunter before the Lord: wherefore it is said, Even as Nimrod, the mighty hunter before the Lord.

10. **Shinar**, i.e. Babylonia.

11. **Asshur** was the name of the original capital of Assyria. In this verse Asshur is said to be the founder of Nineveh.

15. **Heth**. The Hittites were at one time an important power in the country north and north-east of Palestine. Ramses II. (c. 1300-1234 B.C.) made a treaty with them. But the expressions Canaanites, Amorites, and Hittites are all used to denote generally the inhabitants of Canaan occupying the country before the arrival of the Hebrews.

story of Babel, the writer confines himself to the descendants of Shem, the Semitic stock, and more particularly the branch from which the Israelites sprang.

A few notes are added on some points in ch. 10. which are worth special attention.

THE STORY OF BABEL, AND THE ORIGIN OF
THE LANGUAGES OF THE EARTH
Genesis 11:1-9

11:1. And the whole earth was of one language, and of one speech. 2. And it came to pass, as they journeyed from the east, that they found a plain in the land of Shinar; and they dwelt there. 3. And they said one to another. Go to, let us make brick, and burn them thoroughly. And they had brick for stone, and slime had they for mortar. 4. And they said, Go to, let us build us a city and a tower, whose top may reach unto heaven; and let us make us a name, lest we be scattered abroad upon the face of the whole earth. 5. And the Lord came down to see the city and the tower, which the children of men builded. 6. And the Lord said, Behold, the people is one, and they have all one language; and this they begin to do: and now nothing will be restrained from them, which they have imagined to do. 7. Go to, let us go down, and there confound their language, that they may not understand one another's speech. 8. So the Lord scattered

For a full discussion of the whole chapter and its difficulties, see Driver, *ad loc.*

2. **Shinar** = Babylonia.

3. In Babylonia brick cemented with bitumen (A.V. "slime") was the regular material for building.

7. **us**. See on 1:26.

them abroad from thence upon the face of all the earth: and they left off to build the city. 9. Therefore is the name of it called Babel; because the Lord did there confound the language of all the earth: and from thence did the Lord scatter them abroad upon the face of all the earth.

9. Babel = Babylon. As so often with Hebrew names, a false derivation is given, due to the resemblance of two words. Babel, which properly means "gate of God," is here connected with a verb meaning "to confound."

PART II

THE ORIGIN OF ISRAEL: STORIES OF

THE PATRIARCHS

ABRAHAM

His life—The life of Abraham as told in Genesis is not complete; particular episodes have been selected from different sources. But a short analysis is useful as an aid to the memory.

I. Abram and Sarai.

    (i) Ur of the Chaldees; Abram marries Sarai.

    (ii) Haran.

    (iii) Palestine; Shechem and Beth-el.

    (iv) Egypt.

    (v) Hebron (after separation from Lot).

    (vi) Rescue of Lot; episode of Melchizedek.

    (vii) Birth of Ishmael.

II. Abraham and Sarah.

    (i) Destruction of Sodom and Gomorrah.

    (ii) Gerar.

    (iii) Birth of Isaac; expulsion of Hagar and Ishmael.

    (iv) "Sacrifice" of Isaac.

    (v) Death of Sarah.

    (vi) Marriage of Isaac to Rebekah.

    (vii) Death of Abraham.

It will be seen that the first division is mainly based on place-names, and the second on events in Abraham's family history.

Features of the story—1. On no less than eight occasions was a promise made by God to Abraham: and the Hebrews, "the seed of Abraham," attached the greatest importance to these as the foundation of their hopes as a nation. 2. The sacrifice of Isaac "fulfils the twofold object of giving the crowning proof of Abraham's absolute faith in Jehovah, and, further, of demonstrating the moral superiority of faith in Jehovah over the religious customs of other Semitic races." (Hastings' *Dictionary of the Bible,* S. V. "Abraham"). 3. Abraham is regarded as the ancestor, not only of the Hebrews, but also, through Ishmael, of some wandering tribes to the south of Palestine.

The character of Abraham—In spite of obvious difficulties in the story of Abraham, such as repetitions or "duplications" of episodes, and the probability that some passages in his life should be explained as "tribal" legends (i.e. intended to account for the connection between the Hebrews and some other tribe), yet we are convinced that he is a real character of history. He is not colorless like so many of the Greek heroes; his personality is striking and many-sided. He is the founder of the Hebrew race, the "friend" of Jehovah, to whom God gave His promise and with whom God made His covenant; he has all the qualities of a leader of men, and "he was called the Friend of God" (James 2:23). The writer of the Epistle to the Hebrews emphasizes his chief virtue, faith, in a passage which should be read at length (Heb. 11:8-19). A summary of his life and character may be found in Ecclesiasticus (44:19, 20), in words which deserve quotation as a most fitting epitaph: "Abraham was a great father of a multitude of nations; and there was none found like him in glory; who kept the law of the Most High, and was taken into covenant with him. In his flesh he established the covenant; and when he was proved, he was found faithful." [R.V.]

STORIES OF THE LIFE OF ABRAHAM

Genesis 11:27—23

The Family of Abram: migration from Ur of the Chaldees to Haran—11:27. Now these are the generations of Terah: Terah begat Abram, Nahor, and Haran; and Haran begat Lot. 28. And Haran died before his father Terah in the land of his nativity, in Ur of the Chaldees. 29. And Abram and Nahor took them wives: the name of Abram's wife was Sarai; and the name of Nahor's wife Milcah, the daughter of Haran, the father of Milcah, and the father of Iscah. 30. But Sarai was barren; she had no child. 31. And Terah took Abram his son, and Lot the son of Haran his son's son, and Sarai his daughter-in-law, his son Abram's wife; and they went forth with them from Ur of the Chaldees, to go into the land of Canaan; and they came unto Haran, and dwelt there. 32. And the days of Terah were two hundred and five years: and Terah died in Haran.

Second migration: to Canaan—12:1. Now the Lord had said unto Abram, Get thee out of thy country, and from thy kindred, and from thy father's house, unto a land that I will shew thee: 2. and I will make of thee a great nation, and I will bless thee, and make thy name great; and thou shalt be a blessing: 3. and I will bless them

29. See genealogical tree, p. 69.
31. Haran=Carrhae. Here Crassus was defeated and killed by the Parthians in 53 B.C. The narrative appears to combine two traditions about the origin of Abram's family.

that bless thee, and curse him that curseth thee: and in thee shall all families of the earth be blessed. 4. So Abram departed, as the Lord had spoken unto him; and Lot went with him: and Abram was seventy and five years old when he departed out of Haran. 5. And Abram took Sarai his wife, and Lot his brother's son, and all their substance that they had gathered, and the souls that they had gotten in Haran; and they went forth to go into the land of Canaan; and into the land of Canaan they came.

6. And Abram passed through the land unto the place of Sichem, unto the plain of Moreh. And the Canaanite was then in the land. 7. And the Lord appeared unto Abram, and said, Unto thy seed will I give this land: and there builded he an altar unto the Lord, who appeared unto him. 8. And he removed from thence unto a mountain on the east of Beth-el, and pitched his tent, having Beth-el on the west, and Hai on the east: and there he builded an altar unto the Lord, and called upon the name of the Lord. 9. And Abram journeyed, going on still toward the south.

Abram's visit to Egypt—10. And there was a famine in the land: and Abram went down into Egypt to sojourn

6. **Sichem**, etc. R.V. "Shechem, unto the oak"; R.V. marg., "terebinth." The terebinth is the turpentine-tree, and is like the oak. A.V. "plain" should be "oak" in 13:18, 14:13, 18:1.
the Canaanite. i.e. all the various peoples who occupied Palestine before the arrival of the Hebrews.

7. **altar.** The whole of Palestine was covered with such sacred spots, connected by the Hebrews with the times of the Patriarchs, not many of them, no doubt, taken over from the earlier inhabitants whom they superseded. (See Index, s.v. "Altar.")

8. **Hai** = Ai.

10-20. A similar story is told in ch. 20 of Abraham, and in ch. 26 of Isaac. It is characteristic of oriental duplicity, and is related by the writer without comment, but without approval.

there; for the famine was grievous in the land. 11. And it came to pass, when he was come near to enter into Egypt, that he said unto Sarai his wife, Behold now, I know that thou art a fair woman to look upon: 12. therefore it shall come to pass, when the Egyptians shall see thee, that they shall say, This is his wife: and they will kill me, but they will save thee alive. 13. Say, I pray thee, thou art my sister: that it may be well with me for thy sake; and my soul shall live because of thee. 14. And it came to pass, that, when Abram was come into Egypt, the Egyptians beheld the woman that she was very fair. 15. The princes also of Pharaoh saw her, and commended her before Pharaoh; and the woman was taken into Pharaoh's house. 16. And he entreated Abram well for her sake: and he had sheep, and oxen, and he asses, and menservants, and maidservants, and she asses, and camels. 17. And the Lord plagued Pharaoh and his house with great plagues because of Sarai Abram's wife. 18. And Pharaoh called Abram, and said, What is this that thou hast done unto me? why didst thou not tell me that she was thy wife? 19. Why saidst thou, She is my sister? so I might have taken her to me to wife: now therefore behold thy wife, take her, and go thy way. 20. And Pharaoh commanded his men concerning him: and they sent him away, and his wife, and all that he had.

Return to Canaan—13:1. And Abram went up out of Egypt, he, and his wife, and all that he had, and Lot with him, into the south. 2. And Abram was very rich in cattle, in silver, and in gold. 3. And he went on his journeys from the south even to Beth-el, unto the place where his tent had been at the beginning, between Beth-el and Hai;

4. unto the place of the altar, which he had made there at the first: and there Abram called on the name of the Lord.

Lot's choice of land—5. And Lot also, which went with Abram, had flocks, and herds, and tents. 6. And the land was not able to bear them, that they might dwell together: for their substance was great, so that they could not dwell together. 7. And there was a strife between the herdmen of Abram's cattle and the herdmen of Lot's cattle: and the Canaanite and the Perizzite dwelled then in the land. 8. And Abram said unto Lot, Let there be no strife, I pray thee, between me and thee, and between my herdmen and thy herdmen; for we be brethren. 9. Is not the whole land before thee? separate thyself, I pray thee, from me: if thou wilt take the left hand, then I will go to the right; or if thou depart to the right hand, then I will go to the left. 10. And Lot lifted up his eyes, and beheld all the plain of Jordan, that it was well watered every where, before the Lord destroyed Sodom and Gomorrah, even as the garden of the Lord, like the land of Egypt, as thou comest unto Zoar. 11. Then Lot chose him all the plain of Jordan; and Lot journeyed east: and they separated themselves the one from the other. 12. Abram dwelled in the land of Canaan, and Lot dwelled in the cities of the plain, and pitched his tent toward Sodom. 13. But the men of Sodom Were wicked and sinners before the Lord exceedingly.

God's promise to Abram—14. And the Lord said

6, 7. Two reasons are given why Abraham and Lot should separate.

10. **plain of Jordan**, i.e. the basin containing the lower reaches of the Jordan and the Dead Sea.

the garden of the LORD, i.e. the Garden of Eden.

unto Abram, after that Lot was separated from him, Lift up now thine eyes, and look from the place where thou art northward, and southward, and eastward, and westward: 15. for all the land which thou seest, to thee will I give it, and to thy seed for ever. 16. And I will make thy seed as the dust of the earth: so that if a man can number the dust of the earth, then shall thy seed also be numbered. 17. Arise, walk through the land in the length of it and in the breadth of it; for I will give it unto thee. 18. Then Abram removed his tent, and came and dwelt in the plain of Mamre, which is in Hebron, and built there an altar unto the Lord.

THE WAR OF THE FOUR KINGS AGAINST THE FIVE KINGS

Chapter 14 contains the story of the revolt of five "Kings of the Plain" against the King of Elam and his vassals. Elam, with its capital Susa, lies beyond Babylonia, north-east of the Persian gulf.

There are two points of special interest: one is the probable identification of Amraphel, King of Shinar, with Hammurabi, sixth king in the first dynasty of Babylon, whose reign is placed, roughly speaking, in the last quarter of the third millennium B.C. (c. 2250). He conquered Elam and was a great king, but his importance for us lies chiefly in the fact that the Code of Hammurabi, an elaborate legal system indicative of a very advanced Civilization, was discovered 1901-2, engraved upon a huge block of stone containing, in cuneiform characters, 8,000 words. The

18. **in the plain of Mamre** = "by the oaks of Mamre." In 14:13, 24, Mamre is the name of a person; in 23:17 and other passages, the name of a place.

events related in this chapter must refer to an early period of his
career.

The second point of interest is the meeting of Abram with
Melchizedek, the priest-king of Salem. Nothing is known from
other sources about this man: but Psalm 110:4 says:

The Lord hath sworn, and will not repent,

Thou [i.e. the king] art a priest for ever

After the manner of Melchizedek:

and this verse is applied by the writer of the Epistle to the
Hebrews (5:6, 10: 6:20: 7) to Christ, of whom the mysterious
king of the narrative is taken to be a type. Further, in the offerings
of bread and wine brought forth by Melchizedek the Fathers of
the early Church saw prefigured the Bread and Wine of the Holy
Communion.

The war of the four kings against the five kings—14:1. And
it came to pass in the days of Amraphel king of Shinar, Arioch
king of Ellasar, Chedorlaomer king of Elam, and Tidal king
of nations; 2. that these made war with Bera king of Sodom,
and with Birsha king of Gomorrah, Shinab king of Admah, and
Shemeber king of Zeboiim, and the king of Bela, which is Zoar.
3. All these were joined together in the vale of Siddim, which is
the salt sea. 4. Twelve years they served Chedorlaomer, and in the

1. **Arioch**, a prince who ruled in the south of Babylonia, first the vassal of
Chedorlaomer of Elam, afterwards overthrown by Hammurabi (Amraphel)
of Babylon.

Tidal king of nations. R.V. "king of Goiim" (which means "nations").
Nothing is known of him, or of the sense in which Goiim is used here.

2, 3. The position of the five towns in the vale of Siddim is doubtful; perhaps
they occupied the ground now covered by the shallow lagoon at the extreme
south of the Dead Sea. All were destroyed except Zoar.

thirteenth year they rebelled. 5. And in the fourteenth year came Chedorlaomer, and the kings that were with him, and smote the Rephaims in Ashteroth Karnaim, and the Zuzims in Ham, and the Emims in Shaveh Kiriathaim, 6. and the Horites in their mount Seir, unto El-paran, which is by the wilderness. 7. And they returned, and came to En-mishpat, which is Kadesh, and smote all the country of the Amalekites, and also the Amorites, that dwelt in Hazezon-tamar. 8. And there went out the king of Sodom, and the king of Gomorrah, and the king of Admah, and the king of Zeboiim, and the king of Bela (the same is Zoar;) and they joined battle with them in the vale of Siddim; 9. with Chedorlaomer the king of Elam, and with Tidal king of nations, and Amraphel king of Shinar, and Arioch king of Ellasar; four kings with five. 10. And the vale of Siddim was full of slimepits; and the kings of Sodom and Gomorrah fled, and fell there; and they that remained fled to the mountain. XI. And they took all the goods of Sodom and Gomorrah, and all their victuals, and went their way.

Capture of Lot, and his rescue by Abram—12. And they took Lot, Abram's brother's son, who dwelt in Sodom, and his goods, and departed. 13. And there came one that had escaped, and told Abram the Hebrew; for he dwelt in the plain of Mamre the Amorite, brother of Eshcol, and brother of Aner: and these were confederate with Abram. 14. And when Abram heard that his brother was taken captive, he armed his trained servants, born in his own house, three hundred and eighteen, and

10. **slimepits** = bitumen pits. The Dead Sea is called *Laius Asphaltites*.
13. **plain** = "by the oaks."
14. **brother**, i.e. relation (actually, nephew).

pursued them unto Dan. 15. And he divided himself against them, he and his servants, by night, and smote them, and pursued them unto Hobah, which is on the left hand of Damascus. 16. And he brought back all the goods, and also brought again his brother Lot, and his goods, and the women also, and the people.

Meeting of Abram and Melchizedek—17. And the king of Sodom went out to meet him after his return from the slaughter of Chedorlaomer, and of the kings that were with him, at the valley of Shaveh, which is the king's dale. 18. And Melchizedek king of Salem brought forth bread and wine: and he was the priest of the most high God. 19. And he blessed him, and said, Blessed be Abram of the most high God, possessor of heaven and earth: 20. and blessed be the most high God, which hath delivered thine enemies into thy hand. And he gave him tithes of all. 21. And the king of Sodom said unto Abram, Give me the persons, and take the goods to thyself. 22. And Abram said to the king of Sodom, I have lift up mine hand unto the Lord, the most high God, the possessor of heaven and earth, 23. that I will not take from a thread even to a shoelatchet, and that I will not take any thing that is thine, lest thou shouldest say, I have made Abram rich: 24. save only that which the young men have eaten, and the portion of the men which went with me, Aner, Eshcol, and Mamre; let them take their portion.

Abram's vision, and the promise—15:1. After these things the word of the Lord came unto Abram in a vision,

15. **left hand,** i.e. north, according to Hebrew reckoning, as you face the east.

17. **the king's dale.** Here was erected Absalom's monument (2 Sam. xviii. 18).

18. **Salem** = Jerusalem; cp. Ps. 76:2.

20. **he gave him,** i.e. Abram gave Melchizedek tithes of the spoil.

saying, Fear not, Abram: I am thy shield, and thy exceeding great reward. 2. And Abram said, Lord God, what wilt thou give me, seeing I go childless, and the steward of my house is this Eliezer of Damascus? 3. And Abram said, Behold, to me thou hast given no seed: and, lo, one born in my house is mine heir. 4. And, behold, the word of the Lord came unto him, saying, This shall not be thine heir; but he that shall come forth out of thine own bowels shall be thine heir. 5. And he brought him forth abroad, and said, Look now toward heaven, and tell the stars, if thou be able to number them: and he said unto him, So shall thy seed be. 6. And he believed in the Lord; and he counted it to him for righteousness. 7. And he said unto him, I am the Lord that brought thee out of Ur of the Chaldees, to give thee this land to inherit it.

The token—8. And he said. Lord God, whereby shall I know that I shall inherit it? 9. And he said unto him, Take me an heifer of three years old, and a she goat of three years old, and a ram of three years old, and a turtledove, and a young pigeon. 10. And he took unto him all these, and divided them in the midst, and laid each piece one against another: but the birds divided he not. 11. And when the fowls came down upon the carcasses, Abram drove them away. 12. And when the sun was going down, a deep sleep fell upon Abram; and, lo, an horror of great darkness fell upon him. 13. And he said unto

2. **and the steward**, etc. R.V. "and he that shall be possessor of my house is Dammesek Eliezer." The text is uncertain, and the meaning obscure; clearly, however, Abram's steward, a servant, (verse 3) would be his heir if he died childless.

5. **tell ... number**, the same words in the Hebrew.

9. This passage describes the ceremonial of a covenant: the victims are divided, and the covenanters pass between.

Abram, Know of a surety that thy seed shall be a stranger in a land that is not theirs, and shall serve them; and they shall afflict them four hundred years; 14. and also that nation, whom they shall serve, will I judge: and afterward shall they come out with great substance. 15. And thou shalt go to thy fathers in peace; thou shalt be buried in a good old age. 16. But in the fourth generation they shall come hither again: for the iniquity of the Amorites is not yet full. 17. And it came to pass, that, when the sun went down, and it was dark, behold a smoking furnace, and a burning lamp that passed between those pieces.

The covenant—18. In the same day the Lord made a covenant with Abram, saying, Unto thy seed have I given this land, from the river of Egypt unto the great river, the river Euphrates: 19. the Kenites, and the Kenizzites, and the Kadmonites, 20. and the Hittites, and the Perizzites, and the Rephaims, 21. and the Amorites, and the Canaanites, and the Girgashites, and the Jebusites.

The story of Hagar; Abram takes Hagar; Hagar's flight. 16:1. Now Sarai Abram's wife bare him no children: and she had an handmaid, an Egyptian, whose name was Hagar. 2. And Sarai said unto Abram, Behold now, the Lord hath restrained me from bearing: I pray thee, go in unto my maid; it may be that I may obtain children by her. And Abram hearkened to the voice of Sarai. 3. And Sarai Abram's wife took Hagar her maid the Egyptian, after Abram had dwelt ten years in the land of Canaan, and gave her to her husband Abram to be his wife.

13, 14. Refer to Egypt and the Exodus.
16. **Amorites** = inhabitants of Canaan.
17. **burning lamp**. R.V. "flaming torch."

4. And he went in unto Hagar, and she conceived: and when she saw that she had conceived, her mistress was despised in her eyes. 5. And Sarai said unto Abram, My wrong be upon thee: I have given my maid into thy bosom; and when she saw that she had conceived, I was despised in her eyes: the Lord judge between me and thee. 6. But Abram said unto Sarai, Behold, thy maid is in thy hand; do to her as it pleaseth thee. And when Sarai dealt hardly with her, she fled from her face.

Hagar's vision in the wilderness—7. And the angel of the Lord found her by a fountain of water in the wilderness, by the fountain in the way to Shur. 8. And he said, Hagar, Sarai's maid, whence earnest thou? and whither wilt thou go? And she said, I flee from the face of my mistress Sarai. 9. And the angel of the Lord said unto her, Return to thy mistress, and submit thyself under her hands. 10. And the angel of the Lord said unto her, I will multiply thy seed exceedingly, that it shall not be numbered for multitude, 11. And the angel of the Lord said unto her, Behold, thou art with child, and shalt bear a son, and shalt call his name Ishmael; because the Lord hath heard thy affliction. 12. And he will be a wild man; his hand will be against every man. and every man's hand against him; and he shall dwell in the presence of all his brethren. 13. And she called the name of the Lord that spake unto her, Thou God seest me: for she said, Have I also here looked after him that seeth me?

11. **Ishmael**, i.e. "God heareth." Ishmael (verse 12) is a type of the wandering Arab tribes, of whom he was thought to be the ancestor.

12. **a wild man**. R.V. "as a wild ass among men."

in the presence, etc., i.e. to the east of Israel.

13. **Thou God seest me**. This is the meaning implied in the correct R.V., "Thou art a God that seeth."

14. Wherefore the well was called Beer-lahai-roi; behold, it is between Kadesh and Bered.

Hagar returns; birth of Ishmael—15. And Hagar bare Abram a son: and Abram called his son's name, which Hagar bare, Ishmael. 16. And Abram was fourscore and six years old, when Hagar bare Ishmael to Abram.

The name Abraham—17:1. And when Abram was ninety years old and nine, the Lord appeared to Abram, and said unto him, I am the Almighty God; walk before me, and be thou perfect. 2. And I will make my covenant between me and thee, and will multiply thee exceedingly. 3. And Abram fell on his face: and God talked with him, saying, 4. As for me, behold, my covenant is with thee, and thou shalt be a father of many nations. 5. Neither shall thy name any more be called Abram, but thy name shall be Abraham; for a father of many nations have I made thee. 6. And I will make thee exceeding fruitful, and I will make nations of thee, and kings shall come out of thee. 7. And I will establish my covenant between me and thee and thy seed after thee in their generations for an everlasting covenant, to be a God unto thee, and to thy seed after thee. 8. And I will give unto thee, and to thy seed after thee, the land wherein thou art a stranger, all the land of Canaan, for an everlasting possession; and I will be their God.

The rite of circumcision—9. And God said unto Abraham, Thou shalt keep my covenant therefore, thou, and

14. **Beer-lahai-roi.** *i.e.* "the well of the living one who seeth me."

1. **the Almighty God.** Heb. "El Shaddai." This is the name of God which is found in the Priestly narrative as the name until the revelation of Jehovah to Moses on Mount Horeb.

5. Abram (= Abiram) means "the lofty one is father." Abraham is connected by resemblance of sound, but not by derivation, with a word meaning "multitude."

thy seed after thee in their generations, 10. This is my covenant, which ye shall keep, between me and you and thy seed after thee; Every man child among you shall be circumcised, n. And ye shall circumcise the flesh; and it shall be a token of the covenant betwixt me and you. 12. And he that is eight days old shall be circumcised among you, every man child in your generations, he that is born in the house, or bought with money of any stranger, which is not of thy seed. 13. He that is born in thy house, and he that is bought with thy money, must needs be circumcised: and my covenant shall be in your flesh for an everlasting covenant. 14. And the uncircumcised man child who is not circumcised, that soul shall be cut off from his people; he hath broken my covenant.

The name Sarah—15. And God said unto Abraham, As for Sarai thy wife, thou shalt not call her name Sarai, but Sarah shall her name be. 16. And I will bless her, and give thee a son also of her: yea, I will bless her, and she shall be a mother of nations; kings of people shall be of her. 17. Then Abraham fell upon his face, and laughed, and said in his heart, Shall a child be born unto

Note on the Rite of Circumcision

The rite of circumcision was not peculiar to the Hebrews: it was practiced by almost all the Semitic races, and by the Egyptians before the time of Abraham. The original purpose of the rite is thought to have been an initiation into manhood. The Hebrews differed from their neighbors in performing it early, and in regarding it as the, sign and seal of a sacred covenant with the God of the people whom He had promised to bless.

The outward sign was seen to possess an inner meaning by Jeremiah. St. Paul insisted strongly on the purification of the heart; and in the history of the early Church it was soon decided that circumcision was not to be demanded from Gentile converts to Christianity. (See Jer. 9:25, Rom. 2:28, Acts 15.)

15. **Sarai**: the meaning is unknown.

Sarah, i.e. "Princess."

him that is an hundred years old? and shall Sarah, that is ninety years old, bear? 18. And Abraham said unto God, O that Ishmael might live before thee! 19. And God said, Sarah thy wife shall bear thee a son indeed; and thou shalt call his name Isaac: and I will establish my covenant with him for an everlasting covenant, and with his seed after him. 20. And as for Ishmael, I have heard thee: Behold, I have blessed him, and will make him fruitful, and will multiply him exceedingly; twelve princes shall he beget, and I will make him a great nation. 21. But my covenant will I establish with Isaac, which Sarah shall bear unto thee at this set time in the next year. 22. And he left off talking with him, and God went up from Abraham.

The "Three Men" at Hebron— 18:1. And the Lord appeared unto him in the plains of Mamre: and he sat in the tent door in the heat of the day; 2. and he lift up his eyes and looked, and, lo, three men stood by him: and when he saw them, he ran to meet them from the tent door, and bowed himself toward the ground, 3. and said, My Lord, if now I have found favour in thy sight, pass not away, I pray thee, from thy servant: 4. let a little water, I pray you, be fetched, and wash your feet, and rest yourselves under the tree: 5. and I will fetch a morsel of bread, and comfort ye your hearts; after that ye shall pass on: for therefore are ye come to your servant. And they said, So do, as thou hast said. 6. And Abraham hastened into the tent unto Sarah, and said, Make ready quickly three measures of fine meal, knead it, and make cakes upon the hearth. 7. And

19. **Isaac**, meaning "he laughs" Cp. verse 17.
5. **for therefore**. R.V. "forasmuch as." So too 19:8.

Abraham ran unto the herd, and fetched a calf tender and good, and gave it unto a young man; and he hastened to dress it. 8. And he took butter, and milk, and the calf which he had dressed, and set it before them; and he stood by them under the tree, and they did eat.

Promise of a son to Sarah—9. And they said unto him, Where is Sarah thy wife? And he said, Behold, in the tent. 10. And he said, I will certainly return unto thee according to the time of life; and, lo, Sarah thy wife shall have a son. And Sarah heard it in the tent door, which was behind him. 11. Now Abraham and Sarah were old and well stricken in age; and it ceased to be with Sarah after the manner of women. 12. Therefore Sarah laughed within herself, saying, After I am waxed old shall I have pleasure, my lord being old also? 13. And the Lord said unto Abraham, Wherefore did Sarah laugh, saying, Shall I of a surety bear a child, which am old? 14. Is any thing too hard for the Lord? At the time appointed I will return unto thee, according to the time of life, and Sarah shall have a son. 15. Then Sarah denied, saying, I laughed not; for she was afraid. And he said. Nay; but thou didst laugh.

The doom pronounced on Sodom and Gomorrah—16. And the men rose up from thence, and looked toward Sodom: and Abraham went with them to bring them on the way. 17. And the Lord said, Shall I hide from Abraham that thing which I do; 18. seeing that Abraham shall surely become a great and mighty nation, and all the nations of the earth shall be blessed in him? 19. For

10. **according to the time of life**. R.V. "when the season cometh round," i.e. in a year's time. So also in verse 14.

I know him, that he will command his children and his household after him, and they shall keep the way of the Lord, to do justice and judgment; that the Lord may bring upon Abraham that which he hath spoken of him. 20. And the Lord said, Because the cry of Sodom and Gomorrah is great, and because their sin is very grievous; 21. I will go down now, and see whether they have done altogether according to the cry of it, which is come unto me; and if not, I will know. 22. And the men turned their faces from thence, and went toward Sodom: but Abraham stood yet before the Lord.

Abraham's intercession—23. And Abraham drew near, and said, Wilt thou also destroy the righteous with the wicked? 24. Peradventure there be fifty righteous within the city: wilt thou also destroy and not spare the place for the fifty righteous that are therein? 25. That be far from thee to do after this manner, to slay the righteous with the wicked: and that the righteous should be as the wicked, that be far from thee: shall not the Judge of all the earth do right? 26. And the Lord said, If I find in Sodom fifty righteous within the city, then I will spare all the place for their sakes. 27. And Abraham answered and said, Behold now, I have taken upon me to speak unto the Lord, which am but dust and ashes: 28. peradventure there shall lack five of the fifty righteous: wilt thou destroy all the city for lack of five? And he said, If I find there forty and five, I will not destroy it. 29. And he spake unto him yet again, and said, Perad-

19. I know him, that he will. R.V. "I have known him, to the end that he may . . .", i.e. Jehovah singled out Abraham, and afterwards Israel, for a special purpose.

22. I.e. one of the three, who had spoken before, stayed behind. Cp. 19:1, "and the two angels came" (R.V.).

venture there shall be forty found there. And he said, I will not do it for forty's sake. 30. And he said unto him, Oh let not the Lord be angry, and I will speak: Peradventure there shall thirty be found there. And he said, I will not do it, if I find thirty there. 31. And he said. Behold now, I have taken upon me to speak unto the Lord: Peradventure there shall be twenty found there. And he said, I will not destroy it for twenty's sake. 32. And he said. Oh let not the Lord be angry, and I will speak yet but this once: Peradventure ten shall be found there. And he said, I will not destroy it for ten's sake. 33. And the Lord went his way, as soon as he had left communing with Abraham: and Abraham returned unto his place.

Lot receives the two angels at Sodom—19:1. And there came two angels to Sodom at even; and Lot sat in the gate of Sodom: and Lot seeing them rose up to meet them; and he bowed himself with his face toward the ground; 2. and he said, Behold now, my lords, turn in, I pray you, into your servant's house, and tarry all night, and wash your feet, and ye shall rise up early, and go on your ways. And they said, Nay; but we will abide in the street all night. 3. And he pressed upon them greatly; and they turned in unto him, and entered into his house; and he made them a feast, and did bake unleavened bread, and they did eat.

Violence of the men of the city—4. But before they lay down, the men of the city, even the men of Sodom, compassed the house round, both old and young, all the people from every quarter: 5. and they called unto Lot, and said unto him, Where are the men which came in to thee this night? bring them out unto us. 6. And Lot went out at the door unto them, and shut the door after him, 7. and said, I pray you, brethren, do not so wickedly. 8. Behold now, unto these men do nothing; for therefore came they under the shadow of my roof. 9. And they said, Stand back. And they said again, This one fellow came in to sojourn, and he will needs be a judge: now will we deal worse with thee, than with them. And they pressed sore upon the man, even Lot, and came near to break the door. 10. But the men put forth their hand, and pulled Lot into the house to them, and shut to the door. 11. And they smote the men that were at the door of the house with blindness, both small and great: so that they wearied themselves to find the door.

Escape of Lot from Sodom—12. And the men said unto Lot, Hast thou here any besides? son in law, and thy sons, and thy daughters, and whatsoever thou hast in the city, bring them out of this place: 13. for we will destroy this place, because the cry of them is waxen great before the face of the Lord; and the Lord hath sent us to destroy it. 14. And Lot went out, and spake unto his sons in law, which married his daughters, and said, Up, get you out of this place; for the Lord will destroy this city. But he seemed as one that mocked unto his sons in law.

15. And when the morning arose, then the angels hastened Lot, saying, Arise, take thy wife, and thy two daughters, which are here; lest thou be consumed in the iniquity of the city. 16. And while he lingered, the men laid hold upon his hand, and upon the hand of his wife, and upon the hand of his two daughters; the Lord being merciful unto him: and they brought him forth, and set him without the city.

17. And it came to pass, when they had brought them forth abroad, that he said, Escape for thy life; look not behind thee, neither stay thou in all the plain; escape to the mountain, lest thou be consumed. 18. And Lot said unto them, Oh, not so, my Lord: 19. behold now, thy servant hath found grace in thy sight, and thou hast magnified thy mercy, which thou hast shewed unto me in saving my life; and I cannot escape to the mountain, lest some evil take me, and I die: 20. behold now, this city is near to flee unto, and it is a little one: Oh, let me escape thither, (is it not a little one?) and my soul shall live. 21. And he said unto him, See, I have accepted thee concerning this thing also, that I will not overthrow this city, for the which thou hast spoken. 22. Haste thee, escape thither; for I cannot do any thing till thou be come thither. Therefore the name of the city was called Zoar.

Destruction of Sodom and Gomorrah—23. The sun was risen upon the earth when Lot entered into Zoar. 24. Then the Lord rained upon Sodom and upon Gomorrah brimstone and fire from the Lord out of heaven; 25. and he overthrew those cities, and all the plain, and all the inhabitants of the cities, and that which grew upon the ground.

26. But his wife looked back from behind him, and she became a pillar of salt.

22. **Zoar**, i.e. "Little" (verse 20). See ch. 14:8.

24. **brimstone and fire**. Brimstone is sulphur, and hot sulphur springs are found on the shores of the Dead Sea. The destruction of the cities has been explained as caused by an eruption of petroleum after an earthquake. There is no reason why the story should not represent an historical occurrence.

26. **pillar of salt**. "To the south of the Dead Sea are the salt hills known as Jebel Usdum, the Mountain of Sodom, the Salt Mountain."

27. And Abraham gat up early in the morning to the place where he stood before the Lord: 28. and he looked toward Sodom and Gomorrah, and toward all the land of the plain, and beheld, and, lo, the smoke of the country went up as the smoke of a furnace. 29. And it came to pass, when God destroyed the cities of the plain, that God remembered Abraham, and sent Lot out of the midst of the overthrow, when he overthrew the cities in the which Lot dwelt.

The birth of Isaac— 21:1. And the Lord visited Sarah as he had said, and the Lord did unto Sarah as he had spoken. 2. For Sarah conceived, and bare Abraham a son in his old age, at the set time of which God had spoken to him. 3. And Abraham called the name of his son that was born unto him, whom Sarah bare to him, Isaac. 4. And Abraham circumcised his son Isaac being eight days old, as God had commanded him. 5. And Abraham was an hundred years old, when his son Isaac was born unto him.

6. And Sarah said, God hath made me to laugh, so that all that hear will laugh with me. 7. And she said, Who would have said unto Abraham, that Sarah should have given children suck? for I have born him a son in his old age. 8. And the child grew, and was weaned: and Abraham made a great feast the same day that Isaac was weaned.

The casting out of Hagar and Ishmael—9. And Sarah saw the son of Hagar the Egyptian, which she had born unto Abraham, mocking. 10. Wherefore she said unto

(Murray's *Illust. Bible Dict.*: "Salt Sea"). The resemblance to human faces and figures is often to be seen where, as here, the outlines of rocks are much broken. For an account of the whole district, see G. A. Smith, *Hist. Geogr. of the Holy Land*, ch. 23.

9. **mocking**: better, "playing."

Abraham, Cast out this bondwoman and her son: for the son of this bondwoman shall not be heir with my son, even with Isaac, n. And the thing was very grievous in Abraham's sight because of his son. 12. And God said unto Abraham, Let it not be grievous in thy sight because of the lad, and because of thy bondwoman; in all that Sarah hath said unto thee, hearken unto her voice; for in Isaac shall thy seed be called. 13. And also of the son of the bondwoman will I make a nation, because he is thy seed. 14. And Abraham rose up early in the morning, and took bread, and a bottle of water, and gave it unto Hagar, putting it on her shoulder, and the child, and sent her away: and she departed, and wandered in the wilderness of Beer-sheba. 15. And the water was spent in the bottle, and she cast the child under one of the shrubs. 16. And she went, and sat her down over against him a good way off, as it were a bowshot: for she said, Let me not see the death of the child. And she sat over against him, and lift up her voice, and wept. 17. And God heard the voice of the lad; and the angel of God called to Hagar out of heaven, and said unto her, What aileth thee, Hagar? fear not; for God hath heard the voice of the lad where he is. 18. Arise, lift up the lad, and hold him in thine hand; for I will make him a great nation. 19. And God opened her eyes, and she saw a well of water; and she went, and filled the bottle with water, and gave the lad drink. 20. And God was with the lad; and he grew, and dwelt in the wilderness,

12. **in Isaac shall thy seed be called**, i.e. not Ishmael, but Isaac and his descendants, should be the true "seed of Abraham." See Rom. 9:7 seq.

14. **bottle**, i.e. a skin, or leather bottle.

17. **God heard**. See on 16:11.

and became an archer. 21. And he dwelt in the wilderness of Paran: and his mother took him a wife out of the land of Egypt.

The Covenant at Beersheba between Abraham and Abimelech the Philistine—22. And it came to pass at that time, that Abimelech and Phichol the chief captain of his host spake unto Abraham, saying, God is with thee in all that thou doest: 23. now therefore swear unto me here by God that thou wilt not deal falsely with me, nor with my son, nor with my son's son: but according to the kindness that I have done unto thee, thou shalt do unto me, and to the land wherein thou hast sojourned. 24. And Abraham said, I will swear. 25. And Abraham reproved Abimelech because of a well of water, which Abimelech's servants had violently taken away. 26. And Abimelech said, I wot not who hath done this thing: neither didst thou tell me, neither yet heard I of it, but today. 27. And Abraham took sheep and oxen, and gave them unto Abimelech; and both of them made a covenant. 28. And Abraham set seven ewe lambs of the flock by themselves. 29. And Abimelech said unto Abraham, What mean these seven ewe lambs which thou hast set by themselves? 30. And he said, For these seven ewe lambs shalt thou take of my hand, that they may be a witness unto me, that I have digged this well. 31. Wherefore he called that place Beer-sheba; because

Note on the Story of Ishmael

The historical purpose of the story is to show the origin of the "Ishmaelite" tribes, and their connection with Israel. St. Paul gives it a religious interpretation in Gal. 4:21 seq., which see.

25. well. For the importance of wells in the Holy Land see G. A. Smith, Hist. Geography, p. 76 seq.

31. Beer-sheba. For another version of the origin of the name, see 26:23-33.

there they sware both of them. 32. Thus they made a covenant at Beer-sheba: then Abimelech rose up, and Phichol the chief captain of his host, and they returned into the land of the Philistines. 33. And Abraham planted a grove in Beer-sheba, and called there on the name of the Lord, the everlasting God. 34. And Abraham sojourned in the Philistines' land many days.

The sacrifice of Isaac—22:1. And it came to pass after these things, that God did tempt Abraham, and said unto him, Abraham: and he said, Behold, here I am. 2. And he said, Take now thy son, thine only son, Isaac, whom thou lovest, and get thee into the land of Moriah; and offer him there for a burnt offering upon one of the mountains which I will tell thee of. 3. And Abraham rose up early in the morning, and saddled his ass, and took two of his young men with him, and Isaac his son, and clave the wood for the burnt offering, and rose up, and went unto the place of which God had told him. 4. Then on the third day Abraham lifted up his eyes, and saw the place afar off. 5. And Abraham said unto his young men, Abide ye here with the ass; and I and the lad will go yonder and worship, and come again

32. **Philistines**. In 26:1 Abimelech is called "King of the Philistines." But it is probable that the Philistines had not entered Canaan yet; and, if so, the writer has committed an anachronism.

  33. **grove**. R.V. "tamarisk tree." See on 12:7.

  1 *seq*. Human sacrifice prevailed amongst many of the peoples with whom the Israelites came into contact; but at no period, as far as we know, was it considered legal by those Israelites who kept to their ancestral faith. The supreme test of the character of Abraham was his willingness, in obedience to what he held to be a Divine command, to devote to his God not only what he himself considered most dear, but the son through whom he was to become the father of a great nation. The object of such an offering was in future achieved by the sacrifice of an ordinary victim. See also vol. 2., App. 4, "Jephthah's Daughter."

  1. **tempt**. R.V. "prove."

to you. 6. And Abraham took the wood of the burnt offering, and laid it upon Isaac his son; and he took the fire in his hand, and a knife; and they went both of them together. 7. And Isaac spake unto Abraham his father, and said, My father: and he said, Here am I, my son. And he said, Behold the fire and the wood: but where is the lamb for a burnt offering? 8. And Abraham said, My son, God will provide himself a lamb for a burnt offering: so they went both of them together. 9. And they came to the place which God had told him of; and Abraham built an altar there, and laid the wood in order, and bound Isaac his son, and laid him on the altar upon the wood. 10. And Abraham stretched forth his hand, and took the knife to slay his son. 11. And the angel of the Lord called unto him out of heaven, and said, Abraham, Abraham: and he said, Here am I. 12. And he said, Lay not thine hand upon the lad, neither do thou any thing unto him: for now I know that thou fearest God, seeing thou hast not withheld thy son, thine only son from me. 13. And Abraham lifted up his eyes, and looked, and behold behind him a ram caught in a thicket by his horns: and Abraham went and took the ram, and offered him up for a burnt offering in the stead of his son. 14. And Abraham called the name of that place Jehovah-jireh: as it is said to this day, In the mount of the Lord it shall be seen.

15. And the angel of the Lord called unto Abraham out of heaven the second time, 16. and said, By myself

14. **Jehovah-jireh,** i.e. "the Lord will see, or, will provide." The episode seems to have given rise to a proverbial saying connected with Mount Zion, the meaning of which is made somewhat obscure by the change from the active voice "will see" to the passive "he shall be seen" (R.V. marg.).

have I sworn, saith the Lord, for because thou hast done this thing, and hast not withheld thy son, thine only son: 17. that in blessing I will bless thee, and in multiplying I will multiply thy seed as the stars of the heaven, and as the sand which is upon the sea shore; and thy seed shall possess the gate of his enemies; 18. and in thy seed shall all the nations of the earth be blessed; because thou hast obeyed my voice. 19. So Abraham returned unto his young men, and they rose up and went together to Beer-sheba; and Abraham dwelt at Beer-sheba.

Death of Sarah—23:1. And Sarah was an hundred and seven and twenty years old; these were the years of the life of Sarah. 2. And Sarah died in Kirjath-arba; the same is Hebron in the land of Canaan: and Abraham came to mourn for Sarah, and to weep for her.

The purchase of the Cave of Machpelah—3. And Abraham stood up from before his dead, and spake unto the sons of Heth, saying, 4. I am a stranger and a sojourner with you: give me a possession of a burying place with you, that I may bury my dead out of my sight. 5. And the children of Heth answered Abraham, saying unto him, 6. Hear us, my lord: thou art a mighty prince among us: in the choice of our sepulchres bury thy dead; none of us shall withhold from thee his sepulchre, but that thou mayest bury thy dead. 7. And Abraham stood up, and bowed himself to the people of the land, even to the children of Heth. 8. And he communed with them, saying, If it be your mind that I should bury my dead out of my sight; hear me, and intreat for me to Ephron the son of Zohar, 9. that he may give me the cave of Machpelah, which he hath, which is in the end of his field; for as much money

3. **sons of Heth** = Hittites: see Geographical Index.

1—5

as it is worth he shall give it me for a possession of a burying-place amongst you. io. And Ephron dwelt among the children of Heth: and Ephron the Hittite answered Abraham in the audience of the children of Heth, even of all that went in at the gate of his city, saying, 11. Nay, my lord, hear me: the field give I thee, and the cave that is therein, I give it thee; in the presence of the sons of my people give I it thee: bury thy dead. 12. And Abraham bowed down himself before the people of the land. 13. And he spake unto Ephron in the audience of the people of the land, saying, But if thou wilt give it, I pray thee, hear me: I will give thee money for the field; take it of me, and I will bury my dead there. 14. And Ephron answered Abraham, saying unto him, 15. My lord, hearken unto me: the land is worth four hundred shekels of silver; what is that betwixt me and thee? bury therefore thy dead. 16. And Abraham hearkened unto Ephron; and Abraham weighed to Ephron the silver, which he had named in the audience of the sons of Heth, four hundred shekels of silver, current money with the merchant. 17. And the field of Ephron, which was in Machpelah, which was before Mamre, the field, and the cave which was therein, and all the trees that were in the field, that were in all the borders round about, were made sure 18. unto Abraham for a possession in the presence of the children of Heth, before all that went in at the gate of his city. 19. And after this, Abraham buried Sarah his wife in the cave of the field of Machpelah before Mamre: the same is Hebron in the land of Canaan. 20. And the field,

15. **four hundred shekels of silver**: not in coined money, but weighed out. The value of silver in a silver shekel was 2 s. 9 d., but "the purchasing power was many times greater."

and the cave that is therein, were made sure unto Abraham for a possession of a burying place by the sons of Heth.

ISAAC

Isaac, unlike Abraham and Jacob, was not a wanderer. The most important episodes in his life were those in which he himself played a secondary part, e.g. the trial of Abraham's faith at Jehovah-jireh (22) and the blessing of Jacob instead of Esau (27). There is nothing particularly striking about his personality; his career was an eminently peaceful one.

STORIES OF THE LIFE OF ISAAC

Genesis 24-26

The mission of Abraham's servant to Mesopotamia—24:1. And Abraham was old, and well stricken in age: and the Lord had blessed Abraham in all things. 2. And Abraham said unto his eldest servant of his house, that ruled over all that he had, Put, I pray thee, thy hand under my thigh: 3. and I will make thee swear by the Lord, the God of heaven, and the God of the earth, that thou shalt not take a wife unto my son of the daughters of the Canaanites, among whom I dwell: 4. but thou shalt go unto my country, and to my kindred, and take a wife unto my son Isaac. 5. And the servant said unto him, Peradventure the woman will not be willing to follow me unto this land: must I needs bring thy son again unto the land from whence thou earnest? 6. And Abraham said unto him, Beware thou that thou bring not my son

2. **Put . . . thy hand under my thigh**. Prof. Driver quotes a similar form of oath obtaining among the natives of Australia.

thither again. 7. The Lord God of heaven, which took me from my father's house, and from the land of my kindred, and which spake unto me, and that sware unto me, saying, Unto thy seed will I give this land; he shall send his angel before thee, and thou shalt take a wife unto my son from thence. 8. And if the woman will not be willing to follow thee, then thou shalt be clear from this my oath: only bring not my son thither again. 9. And the servant put his hand under the thigh of Abraham his master, and sware to him concerning that matter.

He reaches Haran—10. And the servant took ten camels of the camels of his master, and departed; for all the goods of his master were in his hand: and he arose, and went to Mesopotamia, unto the city of Nahor. 11. And he made his camels to kneel down without the city by a well of water at the time of the evening, even the time that women go out to draw water. 12. And he said, O Lord God of my master Abraham, I pray thee, send me good speed this day, and shew kindness unto my master Abraham. 13. Behold, I stand here by the well of water; and the daughters of the men of the city come out to draw water: 14. and let it come to pass, that the damsel to whom I shall say, Let down thy pitcher, I pray thee, that I may drink; and she shall say, Drink, and I will give thy camels drink also: let the same be she that thou hast appointed for thy servant Isaac; and thereby shall I know that thou hast shewed kindness unto my master.

10. **for all the goods**, etc., i.e. he took choice gifts for the bride and her parents.
city of Nahor = Haran.

His meeting with Rebekah at the well—15. And it came to pass, before he had done speaking, that, behold, Rebekah came out, who was born to Bethuel, son of Milcah, the wife of Nahor, Abraham's brother, with her pitcher upon her shoulder. 16. And the damsel was very fair to look upon, a virgin: and she went down to the well, and filled her pitcher, and came up. 17. And the servant ran to meet her, and said, Let me, I pray thee, drink a little water of thy pitcher. 18. And she said, Drink, my lord: and she hasted, and let down her pitcher upon her hand, and gave him drink. 19. And when she had done giving him drink, she said, I will draw water for thy camels also, until they have done drinking. 20. And she hasted, and emptied her pitcher into the trough, and ran again unto the well to draw water, and drew for all his camels. 21. And the man wondering at her held his peace, to wit whether the Lord had made his journey prosperous or not. 22. And it came to pass, as the camels had done drinking, that the man took a golden earring of half a shekel weight, and two bracelets for her hands of ten shekels weight of gold; 23. and said, Whose daughter art thou? tell me,

15. Rebekah: the relationship can be clearly shown thus:

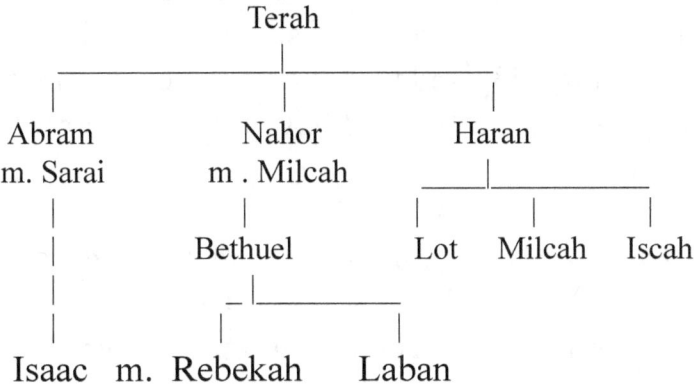

22. **earring**. R.V. "ring." So too in vv. 30 and 47. See note on verse 47.
   shekel. The present value of a shekel of gold is about £2; but see on 23:15.

I pray thee: is there room in thy father's house for us to lodge in? 24. And she said unto him, I am the daughter of Bethuel the son of Milcah, which she bare unto Nahor. 25. She said moreover unto him, We have both straw and provender enough, and room to lodge in. 26. And the man bowed down his head, and worshipped the Lord. 27. And he said, Blessed be the Lord God of my master Abraham, who hath not left destitute my master of his mercy and his truth: I being in the way, the Lord led me to the house of my master's brethren. 28. And the damsel ran, and told them of her mother's house these things.

His reception by Laban and Bethuel—29. And Rebekah had a brother, and his name was Laban: and Laban ran out unto the man, unto the well. 30. And it came to pass, when he saw the earring and bracelets upon his sister's hands, and when he heard the words of Rebekah his sister, saying, Thus spake the man unto me; that he came unto the man; and, behold, he stood by the camels at the well. 31. And he said, Come in, thou blessed of the Lord; wherefore standest thou without? for I have prepared the house, and room for the camels. 32. And the man came into the house: and he ungirded his camels, and gave straw and provender for the camels, and water to wash his feet, and the men's feet that were with him. 33. And there was set meat before him to eat: but he said, I will not eat, until I have told mine errand. And he said, Speak on.

He tells his errand—34. And he said, I am Abraham's servant. 35. And the Lord hath blessed my master greatly; and he is become great: and he hath given him flocks, and herds, and silver, and gold, and menservants, and maidservants, and camels, and asses. 36. And Sarah my master's wife bare a son to my master when she was old: and unto him hath he given all that he hath. 37. And my master made me swear, saying, Thou shalt not take a wife to.my son of the daughters of the Canaanites, in whose land I dwell: 38. but thou shalt go unto my father's house, and to my kindred, and take a wife unto my son. 39. And I said unto my master, Peradventure the woman will not follow me. 40. And he said unto me, The Lord, before whom I walk, will send his angel with thee, and prosper thy way; and thou shalt take a wife for my son of my kindred, and of my father's house: 41. then shalt thou be clear from this my oath, when thou comest to my kindred; and if they give not thee one, thou shalt be clear from my oath. 42. And I came this day unto the well, and said, O Lord God of my master Abraham, if now thou do prosper my way which I go: 43. behold, I stand by the well of water; and it shall come to pass, that when the virgin cometh forth to draw water, and I say to her, Give me, I pray thee, a little water of thy pitcher to drink; 44. and she say to me, Both drink thou, and I will also draw for thy camels: let the same be the woman whom the Lord hath appointed out for my master's son. 45. And before I had done speaking in mine heart, behold, Rebekah came forth with her pitcher on her shoulder; and she went down unto the well, and drew water: and I said unto her, Let me drink, I pray thee. 46. And she made haste, and let down her pitcher from her shoulder, and said, Drink, and I will give thy camels drink also: so I drank, and she made the camels drink also. 47. And I asked her, and said, Whose daughter art thou? And she said, The daughter of Bethuel, Nahor's son, whom Milcah bare unto him: and I put the earring upon her face, and the bracelets upon her hands. 48. And I bowed down my head, and worshipped the Lord, and blessed the Lord God of my master Abraham, which had led me in the right way to take my master's brother's daughter unto his son. 49. And now if ye will deal kindly and truly with my master, tell me: and if not, tell me; that I may turn to the right hand, or to the left.

Rebekah is given into his charge—50. Then Laban and Bethuel answered and said, The thing proceedeth from the Lord: we cannot speak unto thee bad or good. 51. Behold, Rebekah is before thee, take her, and go, and let her be thy master's son's wife, as the Lord hath spoken. 52. And it came to pass, that, when Abraham's servant heard their words, he worshipped the Lord, bowing himself to the earth. 53. And the servant brought forth jewels of silver, and jewels of gold, and raiment, and gave them to Rebekah: he gave also to her brother and to her mother precious things. 54. And they did eat and drink, he and the men that were with him, and tarried all night; and they rose up in the morning, and he said, Send me away unto my master. 55. And her brother and her mother said, Let the damsel abide with us a few days, at the least ten; after that she shall go. 56. And he said unto them, Hinder me not, seeing the Lord hath prospered my way; send me away that I may go to my master. 57. And they said, We will call the damsel, and enquire at her mouth. 58. And they called Rebekah, and said

47. **earring upon her face**. R.V. "ring upon her nose." Cp. "the nose jewels" of Is. 3:21.

49. **turn**, etc., i.e. that I may know what to do.

50. **we cannot speak**, etc., i.e. it is God's doing, and it is not for us to make any comment.

unto her, Wilt thou go with this man? And she said, I will go. 59. And they sent away Rebekah their sister, and her nurse, and Abraham's servant, and his men. 60. And they blessed Rebekah, and said unto her, Thou art our sister, be thou the mother of thousands of millions, and let thy seed possess the gate of those which hate them.

The meeting and marriage of Isaac and Rebekah—61. And Rebekah arose, and her damsels, and they rode upon the camels, and followed the man: and the servant took Rebekah, and went his way. 62. And Isaac came from the way of the well Lahai-roi; for he dwelt in the south country. 63. And Isaac went out to meditate in the field at the eventide: and he lifted up his eyes, and saw, and, behold, the camels were coming. 64. And Rebekah lifted up her eyes, and when she saw Isaac, she lighted off the camel. 65. For she had said unto the servant, What man is this that walketh in the field to meet us? And the servant had said, It is my master: therefore she took a vail, and covered herself. 66. And the servant told Isaac all things that he had done. 67. And Isaac brought her into his mother Sarah's tent, and took Rebekah, and she became his wife; and he loved her: and Isaac was comforted after his mother's death.

The death of Abraham—25:7. And these are the days of the years of Abraham's life which he lived, an hundred threescore and fifteen years. 8. Then Abraham gave up the ghost, and died in a good old age, an old man, and full of years; and was gathered to his people.

60. **possess the gate of** = be victorious over.

62. **the well Lahai-roi**. R.V. "Beer-lahai-roi" The reading of the LXX, "through the wilderness over against the well of the vision," makes better sense. Cp. Gen. 16:14.

8. **his people**. See 37:35, and note.

9. And his sons Isaac and Ishmael buried him in the cave of Machpelah, in the field of Ephron the son of Zohar the Hittite, which is before Mamre; 10. the field which Abraham purchased of the sons of Heth: there was Abraham buried, and Sarah his wife. 11. And it came to pass after the death of Abraham, that God blessed his son Isaac; and Isaac dwelt by the well Lahai-roi.

Esau and Jacob: Esau sells his birthright—19. And these are the generations of Isaac, Abraham's son: Abraham begat Isaac: 20. and Isaac was forty years old when he took Rebekah to wife, the daughter of Bethuel the Syrian of Padan-aram, the sister to Laban the Syrian. 21. And Isaac intreated the Lord for his wife, because she was barren: and the Lord was intreated of him, and Rebekah his wife conceived. 22. And the children struggled together within her; and she said, If it be so, why am I thus? And she went to enquire of the Lord. 23. And the Lord said unto her, Two nations are in thy womb, and two manner of people shall be separated from thy bowels; and the one people shall be stronger than the other people; and the elder shall serve the younger. 24. And when her days to be delivered were fulfilled, behold, there were twins in her womb. 25. And the first came out red, all over like an hairy garment; and they called his name Esau. 26. And after that came his brother out, and his hand took hold on Esau's heel; and his name

20. **Syrian** = Aramaean.

22. *enquire of the LORD*, i.e. at some holy place, just as the ancient Greeks consulted an oracle.

23. The four sentences of the Divine response form a four-line stanza. The two sons of Isaac and Rebekah were to be the ancestors of two nations, Esau of Edom, and Jacob of Israel, and Edom was to serve Israel.

was called Jacob: and Isaac was threescore years old when she bare them. 27. And the boys grew: and Esau was a cunning hunter, a man of the field; and Jacob was a plain man, dwelling in tents. 28. And Isaac loved Esau, because he did eat of his venison: but Rebekah loved Jacob.

29. And Jacob sod pottage: and Esau came from the field, and he was faint: 30. and Esau said to Jacob, Feed me, I pray thee, with that same red pottage; for I am faint: therefore was his name called Edom. 31. And Jacob said, Sell me this day thy birthright. 32. And Esau said, Behold, I am at the point to die: and what profit shall this birthright do to me? 33. And Jacob said, Swear to me this day; and he sware unto him: and
he sold his birthright unto Jacob. 34. Then Jacob gave Esau bread and pottage of lentiles; and he did eat and drink, and rose up, and went his way: thus Esau despised his birthright.

Isaac goes to Gerar—26:1. And there was a famine in the land, beside the first famine that was in the days of Abraham. And Isaac went unto Abimelech king of the Philistines unto Gerar. 2. And the Lord appeared unto him, and said, Go not down into Egypt; dwell in

26. **Jacob**, i.e., "one that takes by the heel or supplants"

27. **plain**, i.e. content with a quiet pastoral life—a contrast to Esau, who was a nomad hunter.

29. **sod**: past tense of seethe, to boil.

30. **Edom**, i.e., Red. As usual, the writer draws attention to a similarity-in the Hebrew words. There is always a picturesque suggestion in this "playing upon words," even if it is not supported by etymology. It has been pointed out that the cliffs of Edom are red.

31. **birthright**. Apparently the right of the first-born to the usual double portion (cp. Deut. 21:17, 2 Kings 2:9) might be sold.

34. **lentiles**. The seeds of the lentil are brown; flour is made of them in Egypt, and they are eaten stewed with other ingredients, such as onions.

the land which I shall tell thee of: 3. sojourn in this land, and I will be with thee, and will bless thee; for unto thee, and unto thy seed, I will give all these countries, and I will perform the oath which I sware unto Abraham thy father; 4. and I will make thy seed to multiply as the stars of heaven, and will give unto thy seed all these countries; and in thy seed shall all the nations of the earth be blessed; 5. because that Abraham obeyed my voice, and kept my charge, my commandments, my statutes, and my laws.

His prosperity there excites envy—12. Then Isaac sowed in that land, and received in the same year an hundredfold: and the Lord blessed him. 13. And the man waxed great, and went forward, and grew until he became very great: 14. for he had possession of flocks, and possession of herds, and great store of servants: and the Philistines envied him. 15. For all the wells which his father's servants had digged in the days of Abraham his father, the Philistines had stopped them, and filled them with earth. 16. And Abimelech said unto Isaac, Go from us; for thou art much mightier than we.

He leaves Gerar, and moves to Beer-sheba—17. And Isaac departed thence, and pitched his tent in the valley of Gerar, and dwelt there. 18. And Isaac digged again the wells of water, which they had digged in the days of Abraham his father; for the Philistines had stopped them after the death of Abraham: and he called their names after the names by which his father had called them. 19. And Isaac's servants digged in the valley, and found there a well of springing water. 20. And the herdmen of Gerar did strive with Isaac's herdmen, saying, The water is ours: and he called the name of the well

Esek; because they strove with him. 21. And they digged another well, and strove for that also: and he called the name of it Sitnah. 22. And he removed from thence, and digged another well; and for that they strove not: and he called the name of it Rehoboth; and he said, For now the Lord hath made room for us, and we shall be fruitful in the land. 23. And he went up from thence to Beer-sheba. 24. And the Lord appeared unto him the same night, and said, I am the God of Abraham thy father: fear not, for I am with thee, and will bless thee, and multiply thy seed for my servant Abraham's sake. 25. And he builded an altar there, and called upon the name of the Lord, and pitched his tent there: and there Isaac's servants digged a well.

Covenant at Beer-sheba between Isaac and Abimelech of Gerar—26. Then Abimelech went to him from Gerar, and Ahuzzath one of his friends, and Phichol the chief captain of his army. 27. And Isaac said unto them, Wherefore come ye to me, seeing ye hate me, and have sent me away from you? 28. And they said, We saw certainly that the Lord was with thee: and we said, Let there be now an oath betwixt us, even betwixt us and thee, and let us make a covenant with thee; 29. that thou wilt do us no hurt, as we have not touched thee, and as we have done unto thee nothing but good, and have sent thee away in peace: thou art now the blessed of the Lord. 30. And he made them a feast, and they did eat and drink. 31. And they rose up betimes in the morning, and sware

20. **Esek**, *i.e.*, "Contention"
21. **Sitnah**, *i.e.*, "Enmity"
22. **Rehoboth**, *i.e.*, "Broad places" or, "Room."

one to another: and Isaac sent them away, and they departed from him in peace. 32. And it came to pass the same day, that Isaac's servants came, and told him concerning the well which they had digged, and said unto him, We have found water. 33. And he called it Shebah: therefore the name of the city is Beer-sheba unto this day.

JACOB

His life—The story of Jacob may be analyzed thus:

A. Early years.
   1. Birth.
   2. Shepherd life.
   3. Supplants Esau in birthright and blessing.
   4. Two motives for visit to Mesopotamia.
      (a) Fear of Esau; (b) to get a wife.
   5. Bethel: vision.

B. Service under Laban: 20 years.
   1. Wins (a) Leah; (b) Rachel.
   2. Returns rich, the father of a large family (oldest, Reuben; youngest, Joseph).

C. Return to Canaan.
   1. Covenant with Laban in Gilead.
   2. Mahanaim.
   3. Penuel; wrestles for the blessing: "Israel."
   4. Meets Esau: reconciliation.
   5. Shechem.
   6. Bethel; sacred pillar.

33. **Shebah**. R.V. "Shibah" (= swearing): see chap. 21:31, The two stories appear to be duplicates of one another.

7. Birth of Benjamin.
8. Hebron; death of Isaac.

D. Migration to Egypt, where he dies. (This division practically belongs to the Life of Joseph.)
1. Story of Joseph and his brethren.
2. Jacob and his family settle in Egypt, in Goshen.
3. Jacob blesses (a) Manasseh and Ephraim, (b) his own sons.
4. Dies: buried in cave of Machpelah.

His character—The character of Jacob is two-sided, and corresponds to the two names, Jacob "the supplanter," and Israel "the perseverer with God" (Hast., *D.B., s.v.* "Jacob"). His rivalry with Esau (*cf.* the historical hostility between the Israelites and the Edomites); the underhand way in which he obtained both birthright and blessing, which ought to have belonged to his elder brother; his cunning, which he showed in many ways in dealing with Esau and Laban; his love of wealth; and, finally, his weakness in dealing with his sons—all these faults are fully emphasized in the narrative, so that we are inclined to despise him and depreciate his character unduly. A man's faults are almost always more obvious than his virtues, and it was so with Jacob. As "Israel," he was a perseverer, a striver, with God; he had a strain of moral earnestness in him, which was totally lacking in Esau, "that profane person" (Heb. 12:16); this is most conspicuous in the scenes at Bethel, Mahanaim, and Penuel; but it can be read between the lines of all his later life down to the moment of his pathetic words to Pharaoh, "few and evil have been the days of the years of my life" (Gen. 47:9).

STORIES OF THE LIFE OF JACOB

Genesis 27-35

Rebekah's cunning scheme to obtain Isaac's blessing for the younger son—27. 1. And it came to pass, that when Isaac was old, and his eyes were dim, so that he could not see, he called Esau his eldest son, and said unto him, My son: and he said unto him, Behold, here am I. 2. And he said, Behold now, I am old, I know not the day of my death: 3. now therefore take, I pray thee, thy weapons, thy quiver and thy bow, and go out to the field, and take me some venison; 4. and make me savory meat, such as I love, and bring it to me, that I may eat; that my soul may bless thee before I die. 5. And Rebekah heard when Isaac spake to Esau his son. And Esau went to the field to hunt for venison, and to bring it.

6. And Rebekah spake unto Jacob her son, saying. Behold, I heard thy father speak unto Esau thy brother, saying, 7. Bring me venison, and make me savory meat, that I may eat, and bless thee before the Lord before my death. 8. Now therefore, my son, obey my voice according to that which I command thee. 9. Go now to the flock, and fetch me from thence two good kids of the goats; and I will make them savory meat for thy father, such as he loveth: 10. and thou shalt bring it to thy father, that he may eat, and that he may bless thee before his death. 11. And Jacob said to Rebekah his mother, Behold, Esau my brother is a hairy man, and I am a smooth man: 12. my father peradventure will feel me, and I shall seem to him as a deceiver; and I shall bring a curse upon me, and not a blessing. 13. And his mother said unto him, Upon me be thy curse, my son:

only obey my voice, and go fetch me them. 14. And he went, and fetched, and brought them to his mother: and his mother made savoury meat, such as his father loved. 15. And Rebekah took goodly raiment of her eldest son Esau, which were with her in the house, and put them upon Jacob her younger son: 16. and she put the skins of the kids of the goats upon his hands, and upon the smooth of his neck: 17. and she gave the savory meat and the bread, which she had prepared, into the hand of her son Jacob.

Jacob obtains the blessing—18. And he came unto his father, and said, My father: and he said, Here am I; who art thou, my son? 19. And Jacob said unto his father, I am Esau thy firstborn; I have done according as thou badest me: arise, I pray thee, sit and eat of my venison, that thy soul may bless me. 20. And Isaac said unto his son, How is it that thou hast found it so quickly, my son? And he said, Because the Lord thy God brought it to me. 21. And Isaac said unto Jacob, Come near, I pray thee, that I may feel thee, my son, whether thou be my very son Esau or not. 22. And Jacob went near unto Isaac his father; and he felt him, and said, The voice is Jacob's voice, but the hands are the hands of Esau. 23. And he discerned him not, because his hands were hairy, as his brother Esau's hands: so he blessed him. 24. And he said, Art thou my very son Esau? And he said, I am. 25. And he said, Bring it near to me, and I will eat of my son's venison, that my soul may bless thee. And he brought it near to him, and he did eat: and he brought him wine, and he drank. 26. And his father Isaac said unto him, Come near now, and kiss me, my son. 27. And he came near, and kissed

I—6

him: and he smelled the smell of his raiment, and blessed him, and said, See, the smell of my son is as the smell of a field which the Lord hath blessed: 28. therefore God give thee of the dew of heaven, and the fatness of the earth, and plenty of corn and wine: 29. let people serve thee, and nations bow down to thee: be lord over thy brethren, and let thy mother's sons bow down to thee: cursed be every one that curseth thee, and blessed be he that blesseth thee.

The grief of Esau, who has been supplanted—30. And it came to pass, as soon as Isaac had made an end of blessing Jacob, and Jacob was yet scarce gone out from the presence of Isaac his father, that Esau his brother came in from his hunting. 31. And he also had made savory meat, and brought it unto his father, and said unto his father, Let my father arise, and eat of his son's venison, that thy soul may bless me. 32. And Isaac his father said unto him, Who art thou? And he said, I am thy son, thy firstborn Esau. 33. And Isaac trembled very exceedingly, and said, Who? where is he that hath taken venison, and brought it me, and I have eaten of all before thou earnest, and have blessed him? yea, and he shall be blessed. 34. And when Esau heard the words of his father, he cried with a great and exceeding bitter cry, and said unto his father, Bless me, even me also, O my father. 35. And he said, Thy brother came with subtlety, and hath taken away thy blessing. 36. And he said, Is not he rightly named Jacob? for he hath supplanted me these two times: he took away my birthright; and, behold, now he hath taken away my blessing.

27. **See**, etc., Isaac's blessing of Jacob is in the form of a poem.
36. **Jacob**. See chap. xxv. 26, note.

And he said, Hast thou not reserved a blessing for me? 37. And Isaac answered and said unto Esau, Behold, I have made him thy lord, and all his brethren have I given to him for servants; and with corn and wine have I sustained him: and what shall I do now unto thee, my son? 38. And Esau said unto his father, Hast thou but one blessing, my father? bless me, even me also, O my father. And Esau lifted up his voice, and wept. 39. And Isaac his father answered and said unto him, Behold, thy dwelling shall be the fatness of the earth, and of the dew of heaven from above; 40. and by thy sword shalt thou live, and shalt serve thy brother; and it shall come

to pass when thou shalt have the dominion, that thou shalt break his yoke from off thy neck.

Reasons for sending Jacob to Mesopotamia—41. And Esau hated Jacob because of the blessing wherewith his father blessed him: and Esau said in his heart, The days of mourning for my father are at hand; then will I slay my brother Jacob. 42. And these words of Esau her elder son were told to Rebekah: and she sent and called Jacob her younger son, and said unto him, Behold, thy brother Esau, as touching thee, doth comfort himself, purposing to kill thee. 43. Now therefore, my son, obey my voice; and arise, flee thou to Laban my brother to Haran; 44. and tarry with him a few days, until thy brother's fury turn away; 45. until thy brother's anger

39. **Behold**, etc. These words of Isaac form a verse. For "of the fatness," "of the dew" the correct rendering of the Hebrew may be "away from": so that the sense of the passage is doubtful.

40. **thou shall break**, etc. cp. 2 Kings 8:20: Edom revolted from Jehoram of Judah c. 849 B.C.

43. **to Laban**. The motive for Jacob's visit to Haran is, according to this chapter, his fear of Esau. In 28 he is instructed to go there by Isaac, who wishes him to choose a wife from the original home of the family.

turn away from thee, and he forget that which thou hast done to him: then I will send, and fetch thee from thence: why should I be deprived also of you both in one day? 46. And Rebekah said to Isaac, I am weary of my life because of the daughters of Heth: if Jacob take a wife of the daughters of Heth, such as these which are of the daughters of the land, what good shall my life do me?

Jacob starts for Haran—28:1. And Isaac called Jacob, and blessed him, and charged him, and said unto him, Thou shalt not take a wife of the daughters of Canaan. 2. Arise, go to Padan-aram, to the house of Bethuel thy mother's father; and take thee a wife from thence of the daughters of Laban thy mother's brother. 3. And God Almighty bless thee, and make thee fruitful, and multiply thee, that thou mayest be a multitude of people; 4. and give thee the blessing of Abraham, to thee, and to thy seed with thee; that thou mayest inherit the land wherein thou art a stranger, which God gave unto Abraham. 5. And Isaac sent away Jacob: and he went to Padan-aram unto Laban, son of Bethuel the Syrian, the brother of Rebekah, Jacob's and Esau's mother.

Marriage of Esau—6. When Esau saw that Isaac had blessed Jacob, and sent him away to Padan-aram, to take him a wife from thence; and that as he blessed him he gave him a charge, saying, Thou shalt not take a wife of the daughters of Canaan; 7. and that Jacob obeyed his father and his mother, and was gone to Padan-aram; 8. and Esau seeing that the daughters of Canaan pleased not Isaac his father; 9. then went Esau unto Ishmael, and took unto the wives which he had Mahalath

46. **daughters of Heth**. i.e. Hittites; see on 10:15.
3. **God Almighty**, Heb. El Shaddai; see on 17:1.

the daughter of Ishmael Abraham's son, the sister of Nebajoth, to be his wife.

Jacob's vision at Beth-el—10. And Jacob went out from Beer-sheba, and went toward Haran. 11. And he lighted upon a certain place, and tarried there all night, because the sun was set; and he took of the stones of that place, and put them for his pillows, and lay down in that place to sleep. 12. And he dreamed, and behold a ladder set up on the earth, and the top of it reached to heaven: and behold the angels of God ascending and descending on it. 13. And, behold, the Lord stood above it, and said, I am the Lord God of Abraham thy father, and the God of Isaac: the land whereon thou liest, to thee will I give it, and to thy seed; 14. and thy seed shall be as the dust of the earth, and thou shalt spread abroad to the west, and to the east, and to the north, and to the south: and in thee and in thy seed shall all the families of the earth be blessed. 15. And, behold, I am with thee, and will keep thee in all places whither thou goest, and will bring thee again into this land; for I will not leave thee, until I have done that which I have spoken to thee of.

16. And Jacob awaked out of his sleep, and he said, Surely the Lord is in this place; and I knew it not. 17. And he was afraid, and said, How dreadful is this place! this is none other but the house of God, and this is the gate of heaven. 18. And Jacob rose up early in the morning, and took the stone that he had put for his pillows, and set it up for a pillar, and poured oil upon the top of it. 19. And he called the name of that place Beth-el:

19. **Beth-el**. i.e., "the house of God." The Hebrew word for pillar, *mazzebah*, means a sacred stone in which the deity was thought to be present.

but the name of that city was called Luz at the first. 20. And Jacob vowed a vow, saying, If God will be with me, and will keep me in this way that I go, and will give me bread to eat, and raiment to put on, 21. so that I come again to my father's house in peace; then shall the Lord be my God: 22. and this stone, which I have set for a pillar, shall be God's house: and of all that thou shalt give me I will surely give the tenth unto thee.

Jacob arrives at Haran—29:1. Then Jacob went on his journey, and came into the land of the people of the east. 2. And he looked, and behold a well in the field, and, lo, there were three flocks of sheep lying by it; for out of that well they watered the flocks: and a great stone was upon the well's mouth. 3. And thither were all the flocks gathered: and they rolled the stone from the well's mouth, and watered the sheep, and put the stone again upon the well's mouth in his place. 4. And Jacob said unto them, My brethren, whence be ye? And they said, Of Haran are we. 5. And he said unto them, Know ye Laban the son of Nahor? And they said, We know him. 6. And he said unto them, Is he well? And they said, He is well: and, behold, Rachel his daughter cometh with the sheep. 7. And he said, Lo, it is yet high day, neither is it time that the cattle should be gathered together: water ye the sheep, and go and feed them. 8. And they said, We cannot, until all the flocks be gathered together, and till they roll the stone from the well's mouth; then we water the sheep.

Note the anointing of the stone and the promise of tithes. The episode is interesting in its bearing on the religious development of Jacob's character, and also because it shows the primitive nature of religious ideas at the time,

He meets Rachel at the Well—9. And while he yet spake with them, Rachel came with her father's sheep: for she kept them. 10. And it came to pass, when Jacob saw Rachel the daughter of Laban his mother's brother, and the sheep of Laban his mother's brother, that Jacob went near, and rolled the stone from the well's mouth, and watered the flock of Laban his mother's brother. 11. And Jacob kissed Rachel, and lifted up his voice, and wept. 12. And Jacob told Rachel that he was her father's brother, and that he was Rebekah's son: and she ran and told her father. 13. And it came to pass, when Laban heard the tidings of Jacob his sister's son, that he ran to meet him, and embraced him, and kissed him, and brought him to his house. And he told Laban all these things. 14. And Laban said to him, Surely thou art my bone and my flesh. And he abode with him the space of a month.

He marries Leah and Rachel—15. And Laban said unto Jacob, Because thou art my brother, shouldest thou therefore serve me for nought? tell me, what shall thy wages be? 16. And Laban had two daughters: the name of the elder was Leah, and the name of the younger was Rachel. 17. Leah was tender eyed; but Rachel was beautiful and well favored. 18. And Jacob loved Rachel; and said, I will serve thee seven years for Rachel thy younger daughter. 19. And Laban said, It is better that I give her to thee, than that I should give her to another man: abide with me. 20. And Jacob served seven years for Rachel; and they seemed unto him but a few days, for the love he had to her. 21. And Jacob said unto Laban, Give me my wife, for my days are fulfilled, that I may go in unto her. 22. And Laban

---

17. **tender eyed**, *i.e.,* weak-eyed.

gathered together all the men of the place, and made a feast. 23. And it came to pass in the evening, that he took Leah his daughter, and brought her to him; and he went in unto her. 24. And Laban gave unto his daughter Leah Zilpah his maid for an handmaid. 25. And it came to pass, that in the morning, behold, it was Leah: and he said to Laban, What is this thou hast done unto me? did not I serve with thee for Rachel? wherefore then hast thou beguiled me? 26. And Laban said, It must not be so done in our country, to give the younger before the firstborn. 27. Fulfil her week, and we will give thee this also for the service which thou shalt serve with me yet seven other years. 28. And Jacob did so, and fulfilled her week: and he gave him Rachel his daughter to wife also. 29. And Laban gave to Rachel his daughter Bilhah his handmaid to be her maid. 30. And he went in also unto Rachel, and he loved also Rachel more than Leah, and served with him yet seven other years.

Jacob decides to leave Laban's service—31:1. And he heard the words of Laban's sons, saying Jacob hath taken away all that was our father's; and of that which was our father's hath he gotten all this glory. 2. And Jacob beheld the countenance of Laban, and, behold, it was not toward him as before. 3. And the Lord said unto Jacob, Return unto the land of thy fathers, and to thy kindred; and I will be with thee. 4. And Jacob sent and called Rachel and Leah to the field unto his flock, 5. and said unto them, I see your father's countenance, that it is not toward me as before; but the God of my father hath been with me. 6. And ye know that with all my power I have served your father. 7. And your father hath deceived

1 **glory**, *i.e.* wealth.

me, and changed my wages ten times; but God suffered him not to hurt me. 11. And the angel of God spake unto me in a dream, saying, Jacob: And I said, Here am I. 12. And he said, 13. I am the God of Beth-el, where thou anointedst the pillar, and where thou vowedst a vow unto me: now arise, get thee out from this land, and return unto the land of thy kindred. 14. And Rachel and Leah answered and said unto him, Is there yet any portion or inheritance for us in our father's house? 15. Are we not counted of him strangers? for he hath sold us, and hath quite devoured also our money. 16. For all the riches which God hath taken from our father, that is ours, and our children's: now then, whatsoever God hath said unto thee, do.

He makes his escape—17. Then Jacob rose up, and set his sons and his wives upon camels; 18. and he carried away all his cattle, and all his goods which he had gotten, the cattle of his getting, which he had gotten in Padan-aram, for to go to Isaac his father in the land of Canaan. 19. And Laban went to shear his sheep: and Rachel had stolen the images that were her father's. 20. And Jacob stole away unawares to Laban the Syrian, in that he told him not that he fled. 21. So he fled with all that he had; and he rose up, and passed over the river, and set his face toward the mount Gilead.

Laban pursues and overtakes him in Gilead: the meeting—22. And it was told Laban on the third day that Jacob

19. **images**. Heb. *teraphim*; see verses 30, 34, Judg. 17:5, 1 Sam. 19:13, and Hos. 3:4. These images were household gods, and their use survived among the Israelites long after they had passed through the more primitive stages of belief. (See ref. given above.)

21. **the river**. The Euphrates.

was fled. 23. And he took his brethren with him, and pursued after him seven days' journey; and they overtook him in the mount Gilead. 24. And God came to Laban the Syrian in a dream by night, and said unto him, Take heed that thou speak not to Jacob either good or bad.

25. Then Laban overtook Jacob. Now Jacob had pitched his tent in the mount: and Laban with his brethren pitched in the mount of Gilead. 26. And Laban said to Jacob, What hast thou done, that thou hast stolen away unawares to me, and carried away my daughters, as captives taken with the sword? 27. Wherefore didst thou flee away secretly, and steal away from me; and didst not tell me, that I might have sent thee away with mirth, and with songs, with tabret, and with harp? 28. and hast not suffered me to kiss my sons and my daughters? thou hast now done foolishly in so doing. 29. It is in the power of my hand to do you hurt: but the God of your father spake unto me yesternight, saying, Take thou heed that thou speak not to Jacob either good or bad. 30. And now, though thou wouldest needs be gone, because thou sore longedst after thy father's house, yet wherefore hast thou stolen my gods? 31. And Jacob answered and said to Laban, Because I was afraid: for I said, Peradventure thou wouldest take by force thy daughters from me. 32. With whomsoever thou findest thy gods, let him not live: before our brethren discern thou what is thine with me, and take it to thee. For Jacob knew not that Rachel had stolen them. 33. And Laban went into Jacob's tent, and into Leah's tent, and into the two maidservants' tents; but he found them

31, 32. Verse 31 answers Laban's first accusation, verse 32 his second.

not. Then went he out of Leah's tent, and entered into Rachel's tent. 34. Now Rachel had taken the images, and put them in the camel's furniture, and sat upon them. And Laban searched all the tent, but found them not. 35. And she said to her father, Let it not displease my lord that I cannot rise up before thee; for the custom of women is upon me. And he searched, but found not the images.

Jacob reproaches Laban—36. And Jacob was wroth, and chode with Laban: and Jacob answered and said to Laban, What is my trespass? what is my sin, that thou hast so hotly pursued after me? 37. Whereas thou hast searched all my stuff, what hast thou found of all thy household stuff? set it here before my brethren and thy brethren, that they may judge betwixt us both. 38. This twenty years have I been with thee; thy ewes and thy she goats have not cast their young, and the rams of thy flock have I not eaten. 39. That which was torn of beasts I brought not unto thee; I bare the loss of it; of my hand didst thou require it, whether stolen by day, or stolen by night. 40. Thus I was; in the day the drought consumed me, and the frost by night; and my sleep departed from mine eyes. 41. Thus have I been twenty years in thy house; I served thee fourteen years for thy two daughters, and six years for thy cattle: and thou hast changed my wages ten times. 42. Except the God of my father, the God of Abraham, and the fear of Isaac, had been with me, surely thou hadst sent me away now empty. God hath seen mine affliction and the labour of my hands, and rebuked thee yesternight.

The covenant between Laban and Jacob—43. And Laban answered and said unto Jacob, These daughters are my daughters, and these children are my children, and these cattle are my cattle, and all that thou seest is mine: and what can I do this day unto these my daughters, or unto their children which they have born? 44. Now therefore come thou, let us make a covenant, I and thou; and let it be for a witness between me and thee. 45. And Jacob took a stone, and set it up for a pillar. 46. And Jacob said unto his brethren, Gather stones; and they took stones, and made an heap: and they did eat there upon the heap. 47. And Laban called it Jegar-sahadutha: but Jacob called it Galeed. 48. And Laban said, This heap is a witness between me and thee this day. Therefore was the name of it called Galeed; 49. and Mizpah; for he said, The Lord watch between me and thee, when we are absent one from another. 50. If thou shalt afflict my daughters, or if thou shalt take other wives beside my daughters, no man is with us; see, God is witness betwixt me and thee. 51. And Laban said to Jacob, Behold this heap, and behold this pillar, which I have cast betwixt me and thee; 52. this heap be witness, and this pillar be witness, that I will not pass over this heap to thee, and that thou shalt not pass over this heap and this pillar unto me, for harm. 53. The God of Abraham, and the God of Nahor, the God of their father, judge betwixt

43. Laban's words seem to mean: "All you have is really mine; if we part, I must at least have a guarantee that you will treat my daughters better than you have treated me."

47. **Jegar-sahadutha ... Galeed**. Both words mean "the heap of witness", the former in Aramaic, the latter in Hebrew.

49. **Mizpah**, i.e. "the watch-tower." The word must refer to some height in the hill-country, or Mount, of Gilead. The saying "The Lord watch," etc., expresses the mutual suspicion of two enemies, not the regret of two friends at their approaching separation.

53. **the God of their father**. R.V. marg. or, "gods". The alter-

us. And Jacob sware by the fear of his father Isaac. 54. Then Jacob offered sacrifice upon the mount, and called his brethren to eat bread: and they did eat bread, and tarried all night in the mount. 55. And early in the morning Laban rose up, and kissed his sons and his daughters, and blessed them: and Laban departed, and returned unto his place.

Jacob at Mahanaim—32:1. And Jacob went on his way, and the angels of God met him. 2. And when Jacob saw them, he said, This is God's host: and he called the name of that place Mahanaim.

His scheme to appease Esau—3. And Jacob sent messengers before him to Esau his brother unto the land of Seir, the country of Edom. 4. And he commanded them, saying, Thus shall ye speak unto my lord Esau; Thy servant Jacob saith thus, I have sojourned with Laban, and stayed there until now: 5. and I have oxen, and asses, flocks, and menservants, and womenservants: and I have sent to tell my lord, that I may find grace in thy sight. 6. And the messengers returned to Jacob, saying, We came to thy brother Esau, and also he cometh to meet thee, and four hundred men with him.

7. Then Jacob was greatly afraid and distressed: and he divided the people that was with him, and the flocks, and herds, and the camels, into two bands; 8. and said, If Esau come to the one company, and smite it, then the other company which is left shall escape. 9. And Jacob said, O God of my father Abraham, and God of my father Isaac, the Lord which saidst unto me,

native reading "gods, "together with the use of the plural verb "judge,"may suggest that the God of each branch of the family of Terah was distinct— another characteristic of primitive religion.

    2. **Mahanaim**. *i.e.* "two hosts or companies."

Return unto thy country, and to thy kindred, and I will deal well with thee: 10. I am not worthy of the least of all the mercies, and of all the truth, which thou hast shewed unto thy servant; for with my staff I passed over this Jordan; and now I am become two bands. 11. Deliver me, I pray thee, from the hand of my brother, from the hand of Esau: for I fear him, lest he will come and smite me, and the mother with the children. 12. And thou saidst, I will surely do thee good, and make thy seed as the sand of the sea, which cannot be numbered for multitude.

13. And he lodged there that same night; and took of that which came to his hand a present for Esau his brother: 14. two hundred she goats, and twenty he goats, two hundred ewes, and twenty rams, 15. thirty milch camels with their colts, forty kine, and ten bulls, twenty she asses, and ten foals. 16. And he delivered them into the hand of his servants, every drove by themselves; and said unto his servants, Pass over before me, and put a space betwixt drove and drove. 17. And he commanded the foremost, saying, When Esau my brother meeteth thee, and asketh thee, saying, Whose art thou? and whither goest thou? and whose are these before thee? 18. then thou shalt say, They be thy servant Jacob's; it is a present sent unto my lord Esau: and, behold, also he is behind us. 19. And so commanded he the second, and the third, and all that followed the droves, saying, On this manner shall ye speak unto Esau, when ye find him. 20. And say ye moreover, Behold, thy servant Jacob is behind us. For he said, I will appease

10. **with my staff**, etc., *i.e.* "I left Canaan with nothing but my staff: I return powerful and wealthy."

him with the present that goeth before me. and afterward I will see his face; peradventure he will accept of me. 21. So went the present over before him: and himself lodged that night in the company.

Jacob at Penuel—22. And he rose up that night, and took his two wives, and his two womenservants, and his eleven sons, and passed over the ford Jabbok. 23. And he took them, and sent them over the brook, and sent over that he had. 24. And Jacob was left alone; and there wrestled a man with him until the breaking of the day. 25. And when he saw that he prevailed not against him, he touched the hollow of his thigh; and the hollow of Jacob's thigh was out of joint, as he wrestled with him. 26. And he said, Let me go, for the day breaketh. And he said, I will not let thee go, except thou bless me. 27. And he said unto him, What is thy name? And he said, Jacob. 28. And he said, Thy name shall be called no more Jacob, but Israel: for as a prince hast thou power with God and with men, and hast prevailed. 29. And Jacob asked him, and said, Tell me, I pray thee, thy name. And he said, Wherefore is it that thou dost ask after my name? And he blessed him there. 30. And Jacob called the name of the place Peniel: for I have seen God face to face, and my life is preserved. 31. And as he passed over Penuel the sun rose

20. **accept of me**. R.V. "accept me."

24. **wrestled**. The struggle of Jacob with his Divine adversary unmistakably represents the striving of the lower and higher sides of man's nature.

25. **touched**, etc., i.e. the opponent of Jacob, to end the struggle, crippled him with a touch.

28. **Israel** = "He who striveth with God"; or, "God striveth." See p. 79 for the change of name.

30. **Peniel** = "the face of God."

upon him, and he halted upon his thigh. 32. Therefore the children of Israel eat not of the sinew which shrank, which is upon the hollow of the thigh, unto this day: because he touched the hollow of Jacob's thigh in the sinew that shrank.

His meeting with Esau—33:1. And Jacob lifted up his eyes, and looked, and, behold, Esau came, and with him four hundred men. And he divided the children unto Leah, and unto Rachel, and unto the two handmaids. 2. And he put the handmaids and their children foremost, and Leah and her children after, and Rachel and Joseph hindermost. 3. And he passed over before them, and bowed himself to the ground seven times, until he came near to his brother. 4. And Esau ran to meet him, and embraced him, and fell on his neck, and kissed him: and they wept. 5. And he lifted up his eyes, and saw the women and the children; and said, Who are those with thee? And he said, The children which God hath graciously given thy servant. 6. Then the handmaidens came near, they and their children, and they bowed themselves. 7. And Leah also with her children came near, and bowed themselves: and after came Joseph near and Rachel, and they bowed themselves. 8. And he said, What meanest thou by all this drove which I met? And he said. These are to find grace in the sight of my lord. 9. And Esau said, I have enough, my brother; keep that thou hast unto thyself. 10. And Jacob said, Nay, I pray thee, if now I have found grace in thy sight, then receive my present at my hand: for therefore I have seen thy face,

32. **sinew that shrank**. R.V. "sinew of the hip," i.e. the sciatic muscle.
10. **for therefore** = "forasmuch as."

as though I had seen the face of God, and thou wast pleased with me. 11. Take, I pray thee, my blessing that is brought to thee; because God hath dealt graciously with me, and because I have enough. And he urged him, and he took it. 12. And he said, Let us take our journey, and let us go, and I will go before thee. 13. And he said unto him, My lord knoweth that the children are tender, and the flocks and herds with young are with me: and if men should overdrive them one day, all the flock will die. 14. Let my lord, I pray thee, pass over before his servant: and I will lead on softly, according as the cattle that goeth before me and the children be able to endure, until I come unto my lord unto Seir. 15. And Esau said, Let me now leave with thee some of the folk that are with me. And he said, What needeth it? let me find grace in the sight of my lord.

16. So Esau returned that day on his way unto Seir.

He arrives at Shechem—17. And Jacob journeyed to Succoth, and built him an house, and made booths for his cattle: therefore the name of the place is called Succoth.

18. And Jacob came to Shalem, a city of Shechem, which is in the land of Canaan, when he came from Padan-aram; and pitched his tent before the city. 19. And he bought a parcel of a field, where he had spread his tent, at the hand of the children of Hamor, Shechem's father, for an hundred, pieces of money. 20. And he erected there an altar, and called it El-elohe-Israel.

17. **Succoth**, *i.e.* "Booths."
18. **to Shalem, a city of Shechem**, R.V. "in peace to the city of Shechem."
19. **pieces of money**. Heb. *kesitah*. The value is not known.
20. **El-elohe-Israel**, *i.e.* "God, the God of Israel."

1—7

Jacob comes to Beth-el—35:1. And God said unto Jacob, Arise, go up to Beth-el, and dwell there: and make there an altar unto God, that appeared unto thee when thou fleddest from the face of Esau thy brother. 2. Then Jacob said unto his household, and to all that were with him, Put away the strange gods that are among you, and be clean, and change your garments: 3. and let us arise, and go up to Beth-el; and I will make there an altar unto God, who answered me in the day of my distress, and was with me in the way which I went.

4. And they gave unto Jacob all the strange gods which were in their hand, and all their earrings which were in their ears; and Jacob hid them under the oak which was by Shechem. 5. And they journeyed: and the terror of God was upon the cities that were round about them, and they did not pursue after the sons of Jacob.

6. So Jacob came to Luz, which is in the land of Canaan, that is, Beth-el, he and all the people that were with him. 7. And he built there an altar, and called the place El-beth-el: because there God appeared unto him, when he fled from the face of his brother. 8. But Deborah Rebekah's nurse died, and she was buried beneath Beth-el under an oak: and the name of it was called Allon-bachuth.

He is given the name Israel—9. And God appeared unto Jacob again, when he came out of Padan-aram, and blessed him. 10. And God said unto him, Thy name is Jacob: thy name shall not be called any more Jacob, but Israel shall be thy name: and he called his name Israel. 11. And

4. **oak**. Or terebinth. See on 12:6.

7. **El-beth-el**, *i.e.* "the God of Beth-el."

8. **Allon-bachuth**, *i.e.* "the oak of weeping."

9 *seq*. gives the Priestly explanation of the name Israel. Notice in verse 11 the title El Shaddai: see on 17:1.

God said unto him, I am God Almighty: be fruitful and multiply; a nation and a company of nations shall be of thee, and kings shall come out of thy loins; 12. and the land which I gave Abraham and Isaac, to thee I will give it, and to thy seed after thee will I give the land. 13. And God went up from him in the place where he talked with him. 14. And Jacob set up a pillar in the place where he talked with him, even a pillar of stone: and he poured a drink offering thereon, and he poured oil thereon. 15. And Jacob called the name of the place where God spake with him, Beth-el.

Birth of Benjamin and death of Rachel at Bethlehem— 16. And they journeyed from Beth-el; and there was but a little way to come to Ephrath; and Rachel travailed, and she had hard labour. 17. And it came to pass, when she was in hard labour, that the midwife said unto her, Fear not; thou shalt have this son also. 18. And it came to pass, as her soul was in departing, (for she died) that she called his name Ben-oni: but his father called him Benjamin. 19. And Rachel died, and was buried in the way to Ephrath, which is Beth-lehem. 20. And Jacob set a pillar upon her grave: that is the pillar of Rachel's grave unto this day. 21. And Israel journeyed, and spread his tent beyond the tower of Edar.

Jacob's family—22. Now the sons of Jacob were twelve: 23. the sons of Leah; Reuben, Jacob's firstborn, and Simeon, and Levi, and Judah, and Issachar, and Zebulun: 24. the sons of Rachel; Joseph, and Benjamin: 25. and the sons of Bilhah, Rachel's handmaid; Dan, and Naphtali: 26. and the sons of Zilpah, Leah's handmaid; Gad,

---

18. **Ben-oni . . . Benjamin,** i.e. "the son of my sorrow," and, "the son of the right hand." The right hand was the lucky one.

and Asher: these are the sons of Jacob, which were born to him in Padan-aram.

The death of Isaac— 27. And Jacob came unto Isaac his father unto Mamre, unto the city of Arbah, which is Hebron, where Abraham and Isaac sojourned. 28. And the days of Isaac were an hundred and fourscore years. 29. And Isaac gave up the ghost, and died, and was gathered unto his people, being old and full of days: and his sons Esau and Jacob buried him.

JOSEPH

Life:

A. Early years in Palestine.
   1. At Hebron. His father's favorite; jealousy of his elder brothers.
   2. His dreams of future greatness.
   3. Visit to his brothers at Dothan.
   4. Two accounts of their plot against him:
      (i) Saved from death at their hands by Judah, he is sold to some Ishmaelites.
      (ii) Saved by Reuben, he is put into a pit, whence he is drawn by Midianites.
   5. Taken to Egypt.

B. In Egypt: promotion to high office.
   1. Given charge of the house of Potiphar.
   2. Resists the temptation of Potiphar's wife.
   3. Thrown into prison: interprets the dreams of the Chief Butler and Baker, and thus is
   4. Brought to the notice of Pharaoh. He interprets the king's dreams, and foretells the famine.

5. Pharaoh approves of his schemes, and gives him power to carry them out.

C. His administration in Egypt.
   1. Seven years' plenty; a fifth of the corn stored every year.
   2. Seven years of famine, during which the whole of the land, except that of the priests, becomes the property of the king.

D. The migration to Egypt of Jacob's family.
   1. Owing to famine in Palestine, the sons of Jacob visit Egypt to buy corn. Then follow the stories of the meeting of Joseph and his brothers, the negotiations, and the final disclosure of Joseph's identity, leading to
   2. The settlement of his brethren as a shepherd community in Goshen. After Jacob's death they are finally assured of their forgiveness by Joseph.

E. Death of Joseph. His bones brought out of Egypt at the Exodus, and ultimately buried at Shechem.

Date—The administration of Joseph in Egypt has been thought to have occurred in the reign of Apepa II., one of the Hyksos (or "shepherd") kings. The Hyksos were foreign invaders, perhaps either Semitic or Hittite; they ruled Egypt for five hundred years, c. 2098-1587 B.C. (Cf. however, Driver, *Genesis*, p. 347.)

While as yet no confirmation of the story of Joseph has been afforded by the monuments, the probability of it finds great support in the fact that in many details it agrees with what is known of Egyptian life and customs. (See Murray's *Illust. Bible Dict.*, s.v. "Joseph," p. 430.)

Character—The character of Joseph is simple and

natural, and is unfolded in the ordinary course of the story. Though a "dreamer" and an interpreter of dreams, he was a man of action and a statesman: he was unspoilt by prosperity, and bore no grudge even when time and circumstances combined to give him the amplest opportunity for revenge.

While faithful to his Egyptian master, he never lost his affection for his kinsmen and his country.

His Egyptian policy may be condemned as unscrupulous; but it must be admitted that it was effective, and it may be excused as being consistent with the standard of morality prevailing at the time.

STORIES OF THE LIFE OF JOSEPH

Genesis 37

His youth, and the jealousy of his brothers—37. 1. And Jacob dwelt in the land wherein his father was a stranger, in the land of Canaan. 2. These are the generations of Jacob. Joseph, being seventeen years old, was feeding the flock with his brethren; and the lad was with the sons of Bilhah, and with the sons of Zilpah, his father's wives: and Joseph brought unto his father their evil report. 3. Now Israel loved Joseph more than all his children, because he was the son of his old age: and he made him a coat of many colors. 4. And when his brethren saw that their father loved him more than all

2. **These . . . Jacob**. This formula should begin an account of Jacob's history after Isaac's death: but the compiler here introduces the story of Joseph from his other (i.e. the Prophetical) source.

sons of Bilhah ... of Zilpah, i.e. Dan and Naphtali; Gad and Asher.

3. **a coat of many colors**, or, "a long garment with sleeves."

his brethren, they hated him, and could not speak peaceably unto him.

5. And Joseph dreamed a dream, and he told it his brethren: and they hated him yet the more. 6. And he said unto them, Hear, I pray you, this dream which I have dreamed: 7. for, behold, we were binding sheaves in the field, and, lo, my sheaf arose, and also stood upright; and, behold, your sheaves stood round about, and made obeisance to my sheaf. 8. And his brethren said to him, Shalt thou indeed reign over us? or shalt thou indeed have dominion over us? And they hated him yet the more for his dreams, and for his words.

Joseph visits his brethren at Dothan—9. And he dreamed yet another dream, and told it his brethren, and said, Behold, I have dreamed a dream more; and, behold, the sun and the moon and the eleven stars made obeisance to me. 10. And he told it to his father, and to his brethren: and his father rebuked him, and said unto him, What is this dream that thou hast dreamed? Shall I and thy mother and thy brethren indeed come to bow down ourselves to thee to the earth? 11. And his brethren envied him; but his father observed the saying.

12. And his brethren went to feed their father's flock in Shechem. 13. And Israel said unto Joseph, Do not thy brethren feed the flock in Shechem? come, and I will send thee unto them. And he said to him, Here am I. 14. And he said to him, Go, I pray thee, see whether it be well with thy brethren, and well with the flocks; and bring me word again. So he sent him out of the vale of Hebron, and he came to Shechem.

15. And a certain man found him, and, behold, he was wandering in the field: and the man asked him, saying,

What seekest thou? 16. And he said, I seek my brethren: tell me, I pray thee, where they feed their flocks. 17. And the man said, They are departed hence; for I heard them say, Let us go to Dothan. And Joseph went after his brethren, and found them in Dothan.

Their successful plotting against him—18. And when they saw him afar off, even before he came near unto them, they conspired against him to slay him. 19. And they said one to another, Behold, this dreamer cometh. 20. Come now therefore, and let us slay him, and cast him into some pit, and we will say, Some evil beast hath devoured him: and we shall see what will become of his dreams. 21. And Reuben heard it, and he delivered him out of their hands; and said, Let us not kill him. 22. And Reuben said unto them, Shed no blood, but cast him into this pit that is in the wilderness, and lay no hand upon him; that he might rid him out of their hands, to deliver him to his father again. 23. And it came to pass, when Joseph was come unto his brethren, that they stript Joseph out of his coat, his coat of many colors that was on him: 24. and they took him, and cast him into a pit: and the pit was empty, there was no water in it. 25. And they sat down to eat bread: and they lifted up their eyes and looked, and,

20. **some pit**. R.V. "one of the pits," *i.e.* one of the cisterns used for water or corn.

21. **For Reuben** read *Judah*. There is little doubt that two narratives are interwoven, one Jehovistic, the other Elohistic (see p. 13).

J.: 21, 25 b. ("and they lifted up their eyes"), 26, 27, 28 b. ("and sold .... silver").

E.: 22, 23, 24, 25 a. ("to eat bread"), 28 a. ("and there passed . . . the pit"), 28 c. ("and they brought Joseph into Egypt") 29, 30.

In J. Judah intercedes, and Joseph is sold to Ishmaelites; in E. Reuben intercedes, and Joseph is drawn out by Midianites.

behold., a company of Ishmeelites came from Gilead with their camels bearing spicery and balm and myrrh, going to carry it down to Egypt. 26. And Judah said unto his brethren, What profit is it if we slay our brother, and conceal his blood? 27. Come, and let us sell him to the Ishmeelites, and let not our hand be upon him; for he is our brother and our flesh. And his brethren were content. 28. Then there passed by Midianites merchantmen; and they drew and lifted up Joseph out of the pit, and sold Joseph to the Ishmeelites for twenty pieces of silver: and they brought Joseph into Egypt.

Jacob's grief at the loss of Joseph, who is sold as a slave in Egypt—29. And Reuben returned unto the pit; and, behold, Joseph was not in the pit; and he rent his clothes. 30. And he returned unto his brethren, and said, The child is not; and I, whither shall I go? 31. And they took Joseph's coat, and killed a kid of the goats, and dipped the coat in the blood: 32. and they sent the coat of many colors, and they brought it to their father; and said, This have we found: know now whether it be thy son's coat or no. 33. And he knew it, and said, It is my son's coat; an evil beast hath devoured him; Joseph is without doubt rent in pieces. 34. And Jacob rent his clothes, and put sackcloth upon his loins, and mourned for his son many days. 35. And all his sons and all his daughters rose up to comfort him; but he refused to be comforted; and he said, For I will go down into the grave unto my son mourning. Thus his father wept for him. 36. And the Midianites sold him into Egypt

25. **spicery and balm and myrrh**, *i.e.* resinous substances found in the country of Gilead.

35. **the grave**. Heb. *Sheol*, the name of the abode of the dead, answering to the Greek Hades (Acts 2:27).

unto Potiphar, an officer of Pharaoh's, and captain of the guard.

Joseph with Potiphar; he prospers—39:1. And Joseph was brought down to Egypt: and Potiphar, an officer of Pharaoh, captain of the guard, an Egyptian, bought him of the hands of the Ishmaelites, which had brought him down thither. 2. And the Lord was with Joseph, and he was a prosperous man; and he was in the house of his master the Egyptian. 3. And his master saw that the Lord was with him, and that the Lord made all that he did to prosper in his hand. 4. And Joseph found grace in his sight, and he served him: and he made him overseer over his house, and all that he had he put into his hand. 5. And it came to pass from the time that he had made him overseer in his house, and over all that he had, that the Lord blessed the Egyptian's house for Joseph's sake; and the blessing of the Lord was upon all that he had in the house, and in the field. 6. And he left all that he had in Joseph's hand; and he knew not ought he had, save the bread which he did eat. And Joseph was a goodly person, and well favored.

Potiphar's wife tempts him in vain: her revenge—7. And it came to pass after these things, that his master's wife cast her eyes upon Joseph; and she said, Lie with me. 8. But he refused, and said unto his master's wife, Behold, my master wotteth not what is with me in the house, and he hath committed all that he hath to my hand; 9. there

6. **he knew not ought he had,** i.e. having Joseph as his steward, he left everything to him except the food. The Egyptians would not eat with a foreigner. cp. 43:32.

7. A similar story is told in "The Tale of the Two Brothers" (Petrie's Egyptian Tales, ii. p. 36), written in the reign of Seti II., c. 1214-1209 B.C.

is none greater in this house than I; neither hath he kept back anything from me but thee, because thou art his wife: how then can I do this great wickedness, and sin against God? 10. And it came to pass, as she spake to Joseph day by day, that he hearkened not unto her, to lie by her, or to be with her. 11. And it came to pass about this time, that Joseph went into the house to do his business; and there was none of the men of the house there within. 12. And she caught him by his garment, saying. Lie with me: and he left his garment in her hand, and fled, and got him out. 13. And it came to pass, when she saw that he had left his garment in her hand, and was fled forth, 14. that she called unto the men of her house, and spake unto them, saying, See, he hath brought in an Hebrew unto us to mock us; he came in unto me to lie with me, and I cried with a loud voice: 15. and it came to pass, when he heard that I lifted up my voice and cried, that he left his garment with me, and fled, and got him out. 16. And she laid up his garment by her, until his lord came home. 17. And she spake unto him according to these words, saying, The Hebrew servant, which thou hast brought unto us, came in unto me to mock me: 18. and it came to pass, as I lifted up my voice and cried, that he left his garment with me, and fled out. 19. And it came to pass, when his master heard the words of his wife, which she spake unto him, saying, After this manner did thy servant to me; that his wrath was kindled. 20. And Joseph's master took him, and put him into the prison, a place where the king's prisoners were bound: and he was there in the prison.

Joseph in prison—21. But the Lord was with Joseph, and shewed him mercy, and gave him favor in the sight of the keeper of the prison. 22. And the keeper of the prison committed to Joseph's hand all the prisoners that were in the prison; and whatsoever they did there, he was the doer of it. 23. The keeper of the prison looked not to anything that was under his hand; because the Lord was with him, and that which he did the Lord made it to prosper.

The imprisonment of the king's butler and baker—40:1. And it came to pass after these things, that the butler of the king of Egypt and his baker had offended their lord the king of Egypt. 2. And Pharaoh was wroth against two of his officers, against the chief of the butlers, and against the chief of the bakers. 3. And he put them in ward in the house of the captain of the guard, into the prison, the place where Joseph was bound. 4. And the captain of the guard charged Joseph with them, and he served them: and they continued a season in ward.

Joseph interprets the chief butler's dream—5. And they dreamed a dream both of them, each man his dream in one night, each man according to the interpretation of his dream, the butler and the baker of the king of Egypt, which were bound in the prison. 6. And Joseph came in unto them in the morning, and looked upon them, and, behold, they were sad. 7. And he asked Pharaoh's officers that were with him in the ward of his lord's house, saying, Wherefore look ye so sadly to day? 8. And they said unto him, We have dreamed a dream, and there is no interpreter of it. And Joseph said unto them, Do not interpretations belong to God? tell me them, I pray you. 9. And the chief butler told his dream to Joseph, and said to

1. **butler** = cup-bearer.
5. **each man according**, etc., *i.e.* each dream having its own special significance.

him, In my dream, behold, a vine was before me; 10. and in the vine were three branches: and it was as though it budded, and her blossoms shot forth; and the clusters thereof brought forth ripe grapes: 11. and Pharaoh's cup was in my hand and I took the grapes, and pressed them into Pharaoh's cup, and I gave the cup into Pharaoh's hand. 12. And Joseph said unto him, This is the interpretation of it: The three branches are three days: 13. yet within three days shall Pharaoh lift up thine head, and restore thee unto thy place: and thou shalt deliver Pharaoh's cup into his hand, after the former manner when thou wast his butler. 14. But think on me when it shall be well with thee, and shew kindness, I pray thee, unto me, and make mention of me unto Pharaoh, and bring me out of this house: 15. for indeed I was stolen away out of the land of the Hebrews: and here also have I done nothing that they should put me into the dungeon.

He interprets the chief baker's dream—16. When the chief baker saw that the interpretation was good, he said unto Joseph, I also was in my dream, and, behold, I had three white baskets on my head: 17. and in the uppermost basket there was of all manner of bakemeats for Pharaoh; and the birds did eat them out of the basket upon my head. 18. And Joseph answered and said, This is the interpretation thereof: The three baskets are three days: 19. yet within three days shall Pharaoh lift up thy head from off thee, and shall hang thee on a tree; and the birds shall eat thy flesh from off thee.

The fulfilment of the dreams—20. And it came to pass the third day, which was Pharaoh's birthday, that he

---

13. **lift up thine head**. *Cp*. 2 Kings 25:27, and note the play on words in verse 19.

made a feast unto all his servants: and he lifted up the head of the chief butler and of the chief baker among his servants. 21. And he restored the chief butler unto his butlership again; and he gave the cup into Pharaoh's hand: 22. but he hanged the chief baker: as Joseph had interpreted to them. 23. Yet did not the chief butler remember Joseph, but forgat him.

The dream of Pharaoh—41:1. And it came to pass at the end of two full years, that Pharaoh dreamed: and, behold, he stood by the river. 2. And, behold, there came up out of the river seven well favored kine and fat-fleshed; and they fed in a meadow. 3. And, behold, seven other kine came up after them out of the river, ill favored and leanfleshed; and stood by the other kine upon the brink of the river. 4. And the ill favored and leanfleshed kine did eat up the seven well favored and fat kine. So Pharaoh awoke. 5. And he slept and dreamed the second time: and, behold, seven ears of corn came up upon one stalk, rank and good. 6. And, behold, seven thin ears and blasted with the east wind sprung up after them. 7. And the seven thin ears devoured the seven rank and full ears. And Pharaoh awoke, and, behold, it was a dream. 8. And it came to pass in the morning that his spirit was troubled; and he sent and called for all the magicians of Egypt, and all the wise men thereof: and Pharaoh told them his dream; but there was none that could interpret them unto Pharaoh.

1. **the river**, *i.e.* the Nile. The prosperity of Egypt has always depended on the regularity of the inundations of the Nile. The cow was a sacred animal.

2. **a meadow**. R.V. "the reed-grass."

6. **the east wind**, *i.e.* the Sirocco, a hot wind blowing from the south-east: Cp. Ex. 10:13, 14:21.

8. **magicians . . . wise men**, *i.e.* two of the priestly classes.

Joseph is summoned, and asked to interpret it—9. Then spake the chief butler unto Pharaoh, saying, I do remember my faults this day: 10. Pharaoh was wroth with his servants, and put me in ward in the captain of the guard's house, both me and the chief baker: 11. and we dreamed a dream in one night, I and he; we dreamed each man according to the interpretation of his dream. 12. And there was there with us a young man, an Hebrew, servant to the captain of the guard; and we told him, and he interpreted to us our dreams; to each man according to his dream he did interpret. 13. And it came to pass, as he interpreted to us, so it was; me he restored unto mine office, and him he hanged.

14. Then Pharaoh sent and called Joseph, and they brought him hastily out of the dungeon: and he shaved himself, and changed his raiment, and came in unto Pharaoh. 15. And Pharaoh said unto Joseph, I have dreamed a dream, and there is none that can interpret it: and I have heard say of thee, that thou canst understand a dream to interpret it. 16. And Joseph answered Pharaoh, saying, It is not in me: God shall give Pharaoh an answer of peace. 17. And Pharaoh said unto Joseph, In my dream, behold, I stood upon the bank of the river; 18. and, behold, there came up out of the river seven kine, fatfleshed and well favored; and they fed in a meadow: 19. and, behold, seven other kine came up after them, poor and very ill favored and leanfleshed, such as I never saw in all the land of Egypt for badness: 20. and the lean and the ill favored kine did eat up the first seven fat kine: 21. and when they had eaten them up, it could not be known that they had eaten them; but they were still ill favored, as at the beginning. So

I awoke. 22. And I saw in my dream, and, behold, seven ears came up in one stalk, full and good: 23. and, behold, seven ears, withered, thin, and blasted with the east wind, sprung up after them: 24. and the thin ears devoured the seven good ears: and I told this unto the magicians; but there was none that could declare it to me.

His interpretation of Pharaoh's dream—25. And Joseph said unto Pharaoh, The dream of Pharaoh is one: God hath shewed Pharaoh what he is about to do. 26. The seven good kine are seven years; and the seven good ears are seven years: the dream is one. 27. And the seven thin and ill favored kine that came up after them are seven years; and the seven empty ears blasted with the east wind shall be seven years of famine. 28. This is the thing which I have spoken unto Pharaoh: What God is about to do he sheweth unto Pharaoh. 29. Behold, there come seven years of great plenty throughout all the land of Egypt: 30. and there shall arise after them seven years of famine; and all the plenty shall be forgotten in the land of Egypt; and the famine shall consume the land; 31. and the plenty shall not be known in the land by reason of that famine following; for it shall be very grievous. 32. And for that the dream was doubled unto Pharaoh twice; it is because the thing is established by God, and God will shortly bring it to pass. 33. Now therefore let Pharaoh look out a man discreet and wise, and set him over the land of Egypt. 34. Let Pharaoh do this, and let him appoint officers over the land, and take up the fifth part of the land of Egypt in the seven plenteous years. 35. And let them gather all the food of those good years that come, and lay up corn under the

34. **take up the fifth part**, *i.e.* store up a fifth of the produce.

hand of Pharaoh, and let them keep food in the cities. 36. And that food shall be for store to the land against the seven years of famine, which shall be in the land of Egypt; that the land perish not through the famine.

Joseph's promotion—37. And the thing was good in the eyes of Pharaoh, and in the eyes of all his servants. 38. And Pharaoh said unto his servants, Can we find such a one as this is, a man in whom the Spirit of God is? 39. And Pharaoh said unto Joseph, Forasmuch as God hath shewed thee all this, there is none so discreet and wise as thou art: 40. thou shalt be over my house, and according unto thy word shall all my people be ruled: only in the throne will I be greater than thou. 41. And Pharaoh said unto Joseph, See, I have set thee over all the land of Egypt. 42. And Pharaoh took off his ring from his hand, and put it upon Joseph's hand, and arrayed him in vestures of fine linen, and put a gold chain about his neck; 43. and he made him to ride in the second chariot which he had; and they cried before him, Bow the knee: and he made him ruler over all the land of Egypt. 44. And Pharaoh said unto Joseph, I am Pharaoh, and without thee shall no man lift up his hand or foot in all the land of Egypt. 45. And Pharaoh called Joseph's name Zaphnath-paaneah; and he gave him to wife Asenath the daughter of Poti-pherah priest of On. And Joseph went out over all the land of Egypt.

His prosperity, and his measures for dealing with the famine—46. And Joseph was thirty years old when

43. **Bow the knee**. "*Abrech*," probably an Egyptian word, similar in sound to the Hebrew word meaning to kneel.

45. **Zaphenath-paneah** (R.V.) probably means "the god speaks and he lives."—**On** = Heliopolis, a town near Cairo, where Ra, the sun-god, was worshipped.

1—8

he stood before Pharaoh king of Egypt. And Joseph went out from the presence of Pharaoh, and went throughout all the land of Egypt. 47. And in the seven plenteous years the earth brought forth by handfuls. 48. And he gathered up all the food of the seven years, which were in the land of Egypt, and laid up the food in the cities: the food of the held, which was round about every city, laid he up in the same. 49. And Joseph gathered corn as the sand of the sea, very much, until he left numbering; for it was without number. 50. And unto Joseph were born two sons before the years of famine came, which Asenath the daughter of Poti-pherah priest of On bare unto him. 51. And Joseph called the name of the firstborn Manasseh: For God, said he, hath, made me forget all my toil, and all my father's house. 52. And the name of the second called he Ephraim: For God hath caused me to be fruitful in the land of my affliction.

53. And the seven years of plenteousness, that was in the land of Egypt, were ended. 54. And the seven years of dearth began to come, according as Joseph had said: and the dearth was in all lands; but in all the land of Egypt there was bread. 55. And when all the land of Egypt was famished, the people cried to Pharaoh for bread: and Pharaoh said unto all the Egyptians, Go unto Joseph; what he saith to you, do. 56. And the famine was over all the face of the earth: and Joseph opened all the storehouses, and sold unto the Egyptians; and the famine waxed sore in the land of Egypt. 57. And all countries came into Egypt to Joseph for to buy corn; because that the famine was so sore in all lands.

51. **Manasseh**, *i.e.* "making to forget."
52. **Ephraim**, *i.e.* "fruitful."

The visit of his brethren to Egypt; their rough reception by Joseph—42. 1. Now when Jacob saw that there was corn in Egypt, Jacob said unto his sons, Why do ye look one upon another? 2. And he said, Behold, I have heard that there is corn in Egypt: get you down thither, and buy for us from thence; that we may live, and not die. 3. And Joseph's ten brethren went down to buy corn in Egypt. 4. But Benjamin, Joseph's brother, Jacob sent not with his brethren; for he said. Lest peradventure mischief befall him. 5. And the sons of Israel came to buy corn among those that came: for the famine was in the land of Canaan. 6. And Joseph was the governor over the land, and he it was that sold to all the people of the land: and Joseph's brethren came, and bowed down themselves before him with their faces to the earth. 7. And Joseph saw his brethren, and he knew them, but made himself strange unto them, and spake roughly unto them; and he said unto them, Whence come ye? And they said, From the land of Canaan to buy food. 8. And Joseph knew his brethren, but they knew not him. 9. And Joseph remembered the dreams which he dreamed of them, and said unto them, Ye are spies; to see the nakedness of the land ye are come. 10. And they said unto him, Nay, my lord, but to buy food are thy servants come. 11. We are all one man's sons; we are true men, thy servants are no spies. 12. And he said unto them, Nay, but to see the nakedness of the land ye are come.

Joseph demands the presence of Benjamin—13. And they said, Thy servants are twelve brethren, the sons of one man in the land of Canaan; and, behold, the youngest is this day with our father, and one is not. 14. And Joseph said unto them, That is it that I spake unto you, saying, Ye are spies: 15. hereby ye shall be proved: by the life of Pharaoh ye shall not go forth hence, except your youngest brother come hither. 16. Send one of you, and let him fetch your brother, and ye shall be kept in prison, that your words may be proved, whether there be any truth in you: or else by the life of Pharaoh surely ye are spies. 17. And he put them all together into ward three days. 18. And Joseph said unto them the third day, This do, and live; for I fear God: 19. if ye be true men, let one of your brethren be bound in the house of your prison: go ye, carry corn for the famine of your houses: 20. but bring your youngest brother unto me; so shall your words be verified, and ye shall not die. And they did so.

They leave Simeon as a hostage, and return conscience-stricken—21. And they said one to another, We are verily guilty concerning our brother, in that we saw the anguish of his soul, when he besought us, and we would not hear; therefore is this distress come upon us. 22. And Reuben answered them, saying, Spake I not unto you, saying, Do not sin against the child; and ye would not hear? therefore, behold, also his blood is required. 23. And they knew not that Joseph understood them; for he spake unto them by an interpreter. 24. And he turned himself about from them, and wept; and returned to them again, and communed with them, and took from them Simeon, and bound him before their eyes. 25. Then Joseph commanded to fill their sacks with corn, and to restore every man's money into his sack, and to give them provision for the way: and thus did he unto

22. **his blood is required**, *i.e.* vengeance is demanded for Joseph's death.

them. 26. And they laded their asses with the corn, and departed thence. 27. And as one of them opened his sack to give his ass provender in the inn, he espied his money; for, behold, it was in his sack's mouth. 28. And he said unto his brethren, My money is restored; and, lo, it is even in my sack: and their heart failed them, and they were afraid, saying one to another, What is this that God hath done unto us?

They return to Canaan; Jacob's grief—29. And they came unto Jacob their father unto the land of Canaan, and told him all that befell unto them; saying, 30. The man, who is the lord of the land, spake roughly to us, and took us for spies of the country. 31. And we said unto him, We are true men; we are no spies: 32. we be twelve brethren, sons of our father; one is not, and the youngest is this day with our father in the land of Canaan. 33. And the man, the lord of the country, said unto us, Hereby shall I know that ye are true men; leave one of your brethren here with me, and take food for the famine of your households, and be gone: 34. and bring your youngest brother unto me: then shall I know that ye are no spies, but that ye are true men: so will I deliver you your brother, and ye shall traffick in the land.

35. And it came to pass as they emptied their sacks, that, behold, every man's bundle of money was in his sack: and when both they and their father saw the bundles of money, they were afraid. 36. And Jacob their father said unto them, Me have ye bereaved of my children: Joseph is not, and Simeon is not, and ye will take Benjamin away: all these things are against me. 37. And Reuben spake unto his father, saying, Slay my two sons, if I bring him not to thee: deliver him into my hand, and I will

bring him to thee again. 38. And he said, My son shall not go down with you; for his brother is dead, and he is left alone: if mischief befall him by the way in the which ye go, then shall ye bring down my gray hairs with sorrow to the grave.

Jacob consents to let Benjamin go—43:1. And the famine was sore in the land. 2. And it came to pass, when they had eaten up the corn which they had brought out of Egypt, their father said unto them, Go again, buy us a little food. 3. And Judah spake unto him, saying, The man did solemnly protest unto us, saying, Ye shall not see my face, except your brother be with you. 4. If thou wilt send our brother with us, we will go down and buy thee food: 5. but if thou wilt not send him, we will not go down: for the man said unto us, Ye shall not see my face, except your brother be with you. 6. And Israel said, Wherefore dealt ye so ill with me, as to tell the man whether ye had yet a brother? 7. And they said, The man asked us straitly of our state, and of our kindred, saying, Is your father yet alive? have ye another brother? and we told him according to the tenor of these words: could we certainly know that he would say, Bring your brother down? 8. And Judah said unto Israel his father, Send the lad with me, and we will arise and go; that we may live, and not die, both we, and thou, and also our little ones. 9. I will be surety for him; of my hand shalt thou require him: if I bring him not unto thee, and set him before thee, then let me bear the blame for ever: 10. for except we had lingered, surely now we had returned this second time. 11. And their father Israel said unto them, If it must be so now, do this; take of the best fruits in the land in your vessels, and carry down the man a present, a little balm, and a little honey, spices, and myrrh, nuts, and almonds: 12. and take double money in your hand; and the money that was brought again in the mouth of your sacks, carry it again in your hand; peradventure it was an oversight: 13. take also your brother, and arise, go again unto the man: 14. and God Almighty give you mercy before the man, that he may send away your other brother, and Benjamin. If I be bereaved of my children, I am bereaved.

Second visit of the sons of Jacob to Egypt—15. And the men took that present, and they took double money in their hand, and Benjamin; and rose up, and went down to Egypt, and stood before Joseph. 16. And when Joseph saw Benjamin with them, he said to the ruler of his house, Bring these men home, and slay, and make ready; for these men shall dine with me at noon. 17. And the man did as Joseph bade; and the man brought the men into Joseph's house. 18. And the men were afraid, because they were brought into Joseph's house; and they said, Because of the money that was returned in our sacks at the first time are we brought in; that he may seek occasion against us, and fall upon us, and take us for bondmen, and our asses. 19. And they came near to the steward of Joseph's house, and they communed with him at the door of the house, 20. and said, O sir, we came indeed down at the first time to buy food: 21. and it came to pass, when we came to the inn, that we opened our sacks, and, behold, every man's money was in the mouth of his sack, our money in full weight: and we have brought it again in our hand. 22. And other money have we brought down in our hands to buy food: we cannot tell who put

21. **weight** The Egyptians weighed out rings of gold.

our money in our sacks. 23. And he said, Peace be to you, fear not: your God, and the God of your father, hath given you treasure in your sacks: I had your money. And he brought Simeon out unto them. 24. And the man brought the men into Joseph's house, and gave them water, and they washed their feet; and he gave their asses provender. 25. And they made ready the present against Joseph came at noon: for they heard that they should eat bread there.

Their reception by Joseph—26. And when Joseph came home, they brought him the present which was in their hand into the house, and bowed themselves to him to the earth. 27. And he asked them of their welfare, and said, Is your father well, the old man of whom ye spake? Is he yet alive? 28. And they answered, Thy servant our father is in good health, he is yet alive. And they bowed down their heads, and made obeisance. 29. And he lifted up his eyes, and saw his brother Benjamin, his mother's son, and said, Is this your younger brother, of whom ye spake unto me? And he said, God be gracious unto thee, my son. 30. And Joseph made haste; for his bowels did yearn upon his brother: and he sought where to weep; and he entered into his chamber, and wept there. 31. And he washed his face, and went out, and refrained himself, and said, Set on bread. 32. And they set on for him by himself, and for them by themselves, and for the Egyptians, which did eat with him, by themselves: because the Egyptians might not eat bread with the Hebrews; for that is an abomination unto the Egyptians. 33. And they sat before him, the firstborn according to his birthright, and the youngest according to his youth: and the men marvelled one at another.

34. And he took and sent messes unto them from before him: but Benjamin's mess was five times so much as any of theirs. And they drank, and were merry with him.

His scheme to test them—44: 1. And he commanded the steward of his house, saying, Fill the men's sacks with food, as much as they can carry, and put every man's money in his sack's mouth. 2. And put my cup, the silver cup, in the sack's mouth of the youngest, and his corn money. And he did according to the word that Joseph had spoken. 3. As soon as the morning was light, the men were sent away, they and their asses. 4. And when they were gone out of the city, and not yet far off, Joseph said unto his steward, Up, follow after the men; and when thou dost overtake them, say unto them, Wherefore have ye rewarded evil for good? 5. Is not this it in which my lord drinketh, and whereby indeed he divineth? ye have done evil in so doing. 6. And he overtook them, and he spake unto them these same words. 7. And they said unto him, Wherefore saith my lord these words? God forbid that thy servants should do according to this thing: 8. behold, the money, which we found in our sacks' mouths, we brought again unto thee out of the land of Canaan: how then should we steal out of thy lord's house silver or gold? 9. With whomsoever of thy servants it be found, both let him die, and we also will be my lord's bondmen. 10. And he said, Now also let it be according unto your words: he with whom it is found shall be my servant; and ye

34. **messes**, *i.e.* special helpings.

5. **divineth**. The method of divination by a cup was to throw precious things into the cup and observe the water. Other means of divination in the Old Testament are dreams, Urim, the lot, teraphim—all used by the Israelites to forecast the future.

shall be blameless, 11. Then they speedily took down every man his sack to the ground, and opened every man his sack. 12. And he searched, and began at the eldest, and left at the youngest: and the cup was found in Benjamin's sack. 13. Then they rent their clothes, and laded every man his ass, and returned to the city.

Judah pleads with Joseph—14. And Judah and his brethren came to Joseph's house; for he was yet there: and they fell before him on the ground. 15. And Joseph said unto them, What deed is this that ye have done? wot ye not that such a man as I can certainly divine? 16. And Judah said, What shall we say unto my lord? what shall we speak? or how shall we clear ourselves? God hath found out the iniquity of thy servants: behold, we are my lord's servants, both we, and he also with whom the cup is found. 17. And he said, God forbid that I should do so: but the man in whose hand the cup is found, he shall be my servant; and as for you, get you up in peace unto your father. 18. Then Judah came near unto him, and said, Oh my lord, let thy servant, I pray thee, speak a word in my lord's ears, and let not thine anger burn against thy servant: for thou art even as Pharaoh. 19. My lord asked his servants, saying, Have ye a father, or a brother? 20. And we said unto my lord, We have a father, an old man, and a child of his old age, a little one; and his brother is dead, and he alone is left of his mother, and his father loveth him. 21. And thou saidst unto thy servants, Bring him down unto me, that I may set mine eyes upon him. 22. And we said unto my lord, The lad cannot leave his father: for if he should leave his father, his father would die. 23. And thou saidst unto thy servants, Except your youngest brother come down with you, ye shall see my face no more. 24. And it came to pass when we came up unto thy servant my father, we told him the words of my lord. 25. And our father said, Go again, and buy us a little food. 26. And we said, We cannot go down: if our youngest brother be with us, then will we go down: for we may not see the man's face, except our youngest brother be with us. 27. And thy servant my father said unto us, Ye know that my wife bare me two sons: 28. and the one went out from me, and I said, Surely he is torn in pieces; and I saw him not since: 29. and if ye take this also from me, and mischief befall him, ye shall bring down my gray hairs with sorrow to the grave. 30. Now therefore when I come to thy servant my father, and the lad be not with us; seeing that his life is bound up in the lad's life; 31. it shall come to pass, when he seeth that the lad is not with us, that he will die: and thy servants shall bring down the gray hairs of thy servant our father with sorrow to the grave. 32. For thy servant became surety for the lad unto my father, saying, If I bring him not unto thee, then I shall bear the blame to my father for ever. 33. Now therefore, I pray thee, let thy servant abide instead of the lad a bondman to my lord; and let the lad go up with his brethren. 34. For how shall I go up to my father, and the lad be not with me? lest peradventure I see the evil that shall come on my father.

Joseph discovers himself to his brethren—45: 1. Then Joseph could not refrain himself before all them that stood by him; and he cried, Cause every man to go out from me. And there stood no man with him, while Joseph

30. his life, etc. R.V. marg., "his soul is knit with the lad's soul." See 1 Sam. 18:1.

made himself known unto his brethren. 2. And he wept aloud: and the Egyptians and the house of Pharaoh heard. 3. And Joseph said unto his brethren, I am Joseph; doth my father yet live? And his brethren could not answer him; for they were troubled at his presence. 4. And Joseph said unto his brethren, Come near to me, I pray you. And they came near. And he said, I am Joseph your brother, whom ye sold into Egypt. 5. Now therefore be not grieved, nor angry with yourselves, that ye sold me hither: for God did send me before you to preserve life. 6. For these two years hath the famine been in the land: and yet there are five years, in the which there shall neither be earing nor harvest. 7. And God sent me before you to preserve you a posterity in the earth, and to save your lives by a great deliverance. 8. So now it was not you that sent me hither, but God: and he hath made me a father to Pharaoh, and lord of all his house, and a ruler throughout all the land of Egypt. 9. Haste ye, and go up to my father, and say unto him, Thus saith thy son Joseph, God hath made me lord of all Egypt: come down unto me, tarry not: 10. and thou shalt dwell in the land of Goshen, and thou shalt be near unto me, thou, and thy children, and thy children's children, and thy flocks, and thy herds, and all that thou hast: 11. and there will I nourish thee; for yet there are five years of famine; lest thou, and thy household, and all that thou hast, come to poverty. 12. And, behold, your eyes see, and the eyes of my brother Benjamin, that it is my mouth that speaketh unto you. 13. And ye shall tell my father of all my glory in Egypt, and of all that ye have seen; and

10. **Goshen**, a division or name of lower Egypt, forty miles northeast of Cairo.

ye shall haste and bring down my father hither. 14. And he fell upon his brother Benjamin's neck, and wept; and Benjamin wept upon his neck. 15. Moreover he kissed all his brethren, and wept upon them: and after that his brethren talked with him.

Pharaoh invites the family of Jacob to settle in Egypt—16. And the fame thereof was heard in Pharaoh's house, saying, Joseph's brethren are come: and it pleased Pharaoh well, and his servants. 17. And Pharaoh said unto Joseph, Say unto thy brethren, This do ye; lade your beasts, and go, get you unto the land of Canaan; 18. and take your father and your households, and come unto me: and I will give you the good of the land of Egypt, and ye shall eat the fat of the land. 19. Now thou art commanded, this do ye; take you wagons out of the land of Egypt for your little ones, and for your wives, and bring your father, and come. 20. Also regard not your stuff; for the good of all the land of Egypt is yours. 21. And the children of Israel did so: and Joseph gave them wagons, according to the commandment of Pharaoh, and gave them provision for the way. 22. To all of them he gave each man changes of raiment; but to Benjamin he gave three hundred pieces of silver, and five changes of raiment. 23. And to his father he sent after this manner; ten asses laden with the good things of Egypt, and ten she asses laden with corn and bread and meat for his father by the way. 24. So he sent his brethren away, and they departed: and he said unto them, See that ye fall not out by the way.

Jacob and his house leave Canaan—25. And they went up out of Egypt, and came into the land of Canaan unto Jacob their father. 26. And told him, saying, Joseph is

22. **pieces** = shekels.

yet alive, and he is governor over all the land of Egypt. And Jacob's heart fainted, for he believed them not. 27. And they told him all the words of Joseph, which he had said unto them: and when he saw the wagons which Joseph had sent to carry him, the spirit of Jacob their father revived: 28. and Israel said, It is enough; Joseph my son is yet alive: I will go and see him before I die.

Renewal of the Promise to Jacob at Beer-sheba—46: 1. And Israel took his journey with all that he had, and came to Beer-sheba, and offered sacrifices unto the God of his father Isaac. 2. And God spake unto Israel in the visions of the night, and said, Jacob, Jacob. And he said. Here am I. 3. And he said, I am God, the God of thy father: fear not to go down into Egypt; for I will there make of thee a great nation: 4. I will go down with thee into Egypt; and I will also surely bring thee up again: and Joseph shall put his hand upon thine eyes. 5. And Jacob rose up from Beer-sheba: and the sons of Israel carried Jacob their father, and their little ones, and their wives, in the wagons which Pharaoh had sent to carry him. 6. And they took their cattle, and their goods, which they had gotten in the land of Canaan, and came into Egypt, Jacob, and all his seed w T ith him: 7. his sons, and his sons' sons with him, his daughters, and his sons' daughters, and all his seed brought he with him into Egypt.

Meeting of Jacob and Joseph in Goshen—26. All the souls that came with Jacob into Egypt, besides Jacob's sons' wives, all the souls were threescore and six; 27. and the sons of Joseph,

1. Isaac, *Cp.* 26:25.
4. **put his hand**, etc., *i.e.* close thine eyes in death.

which were born him in Egypt, were two souls: all the souls of the house of Jacob, which came into Egypt, were threescore and ten. 28. And he sent Judah before him unto Joseph, to direct his face unto Goshen; and they came into the land of Goshen. 29. And Joseph made ready his chariot, and went up to meet Israel his father, to Goshen, and presented himself unto him; and he fell on his neck, and wept on his neck a good while. 30. And Israel said unto Joseph, Now let me die, since I have seen thy face, because thou art yet alive. 31. And Joseph said unto his brethren, and unto his father's house, I will go up, and shew Pharaoh, and say unto him, My brethren, and my father's house, which were in the land of Canaan, are come unto me; 32. and the men are shepherds, for their trade hath been to feed cattle; and they have brought their flocks, and their herds, and all that they have. 33. And it shall come to pass, when Pharaoh shall call you, and shall say, What is your occupation? 34. that ye shall say, Thy servants' trade hath been about cattle from our youth even until now, both we, and also our fathers: that ye may dwell in the land of Goshen; for every shepherd is an abomination unto the Egyptians.

They settle in Goshen—47: 1. Then Joseph came and told Pharaoh, and said, My father and my brethren, and their flocks, and their herds, and all that they have, are come out of the land of Canaan; and, behold, they are in the land of Goshen. 2. And he took some of his brethren, even five men, and presented them unto Pharaoh. 3. And Pharaoh said unto his brethren, What is your occupation? And they said unto Pharaoh, Thy servants are shepherds, both we, and also our fathers. 4. They said

34. **shepherd**. Herodotus tells us that the Egyptians also despised swineherds (Herod. II. 47).

moreover unto Pharaoh, For to sojourn in the land are we come; for thy servants have no pasture for their flocks; for the famine is sore in the land of Canaan: now therefore, we pray thee, let thy servants dwell in the land of Goshen. 5. And Pharaoh spake unto Joseph, saying, Thy father and thy brethren are come unto thee: 6. the land of Egypt is before thee; in the best of the land make thy father and brethren to dwell; in the land of Goshen let them dwell: and if thou knowest any men of activity among them, then make them rulers over my cattle. 7. And Joseph brought in Jacob his father, and set him before Pharaoh: and Jacob blessed Pharaoh. 8. And Pharaoh said unto Jacob, How old art thou? 9. And Jacob said unto Pharaoh, The days of the years of my pilgrimage are an hundred and thirty years: few and evil have the days of the years of my life been, and have not attained unto the days of the years of the life of my fathers in the days of their pilgrimage. 10. And Jacob blessed Pharaoh, and went out from before Pharaoh. 11. And Joseph placed his father and his brethren, and gave them a possession in the land of Egypt, in the best of the land, in the land of Rameses, as Pharaoh had commanded. 12. And Joseph nourished his father, and his brethren, and all his father's household, with bread, according to their families.

Joseph's administration of Egypt—13. And there was no bread in all the land; for the famine was very sore, so that the land of Egypt and all the land of Canaan fainted by reason of the famine. 14. And Joseph gathered up

11. **Rameses**. This is an anachronism: Ramses II was the Pharaoh of the Oppression "which knew not Joseph" and according to Ex. 1:11, it was for him that the Israelites built Pithom and Raamses.

all the money that was found in the land of Egypt, and in the land of Canaan, for the corn which they bought: and Joseph brought the money into Pharaoh's house. 15. And when money failed in the land of Egypt, and in the land of Canaan, all the Egyptians came unto Joseph, and said, Give us bread: for why should we die in thy presence? for the money faileth. 16. And Joseph said, Give your cattle; and I will give you for your cattle, if money fail. 17. And they brought their cattle unto Joseph: and Joseph gave them bread in exchange for horses, and for the flocks, and for the cattle of the herds, and for the asses: and he fed them with bread for all their cattle for that year. 18. When that year was ended, they came unto him the second year, and said unto him. We will not hide it from my lord, how that our money is spent; my lord also hath our herds of cattle; there is not ought left in the sight of my lord, but our bodies, and our lands. 19. Wherefore shall we die before thine eyes, both we and our land? buy us and our land for bread, and we and our land will be servants unto Pharaoh: and give us seed, that we may live, and not die, that the land be not desolate. 20. And Joseph bought all the land of Egypt for Pharaoh; for the Egyptians sold every man his field, because the famine prevailed over them: so the land became Pharaoh's. 21. And as for the people, he removed them to cities from one end of the borders of Egypt even to the other end thereof. 22. Only the land

21. **he removed them**. The reading of the Septuagint and the Vulgate is, "he made bondmen of them, from," etc. The stages in the economic change in Egypt were as follows: (1) the people gave all their money, (2) their cattle, (3) themselves and their land, for corn; (4) they were allowed to retain the land on payment of one-fifth, or 20 per cent. This applied to all but the priests.

1—9

of the priests bought he not; for the priests had a portion assigned them of Pharaoh, and did eat their portion which Pharaoh gave them: wherefore they sold not their lands. 23. Then Joseph said unto the people, Behold, I have bought you this day and your land for Pharaoh: lo, here is seed for you, and ye shall sow the land. 24. And it shall come to pass in the increase, that ye shall give the fifth part unto Pharaoh, and four parts shall be your own, for seed of the field, and for your food, and for them of your households, and for food for your little ones. 25. And they said, Thou hast saved our lives: let us find grace in the sight of my lord, and we will be Pharaoh's servants. 26. And Joseph made it a law over the land of Egypt unto this day, that Pharaoh should have the fifth part; except the land of the priests only, which became not Pharaoh's.

Jacob grows old in Egypt—27. And Israel dwelt in the land of Egypt, in the country of Goshen; and they had possessions therein, and grew, and multiplied exceedingly. 28. And Jacob lived in the land of Egypt seventeen years: so the whole age of Jacob was an hundred forty and seven years. 29. And the time drew nigh that Israel must die: and he called his son Joseph, and said unto him, If now I have found grace in thy sight, put, I pray thee, thy hand under my thigh, and deal kindly and truly with me; bury me not, I pray thee, in Egypt: 30. but I will lie with my fathers, and thou shalt carry me out of Egypt, and bury me in their burying place. And he said, I will do as thou hast said. 31. And he said, Swear unto me. And he sware unto him. And Israel bowed himself upon the bed's head.

29. **thigh**. See on 24:2.
30. **their burying place**, *i.e.* Machpelah.

Jacob blesses the house of Joseph—48: 1. And it came to pass after these things, that one told Joseph, Behold, thy father is sick: and he took with him his two sons, Manasseh and Ephraim. 2. And one told Jacob, and said, Behold, thy son J oseph cometh unto thee: and Israel strengthened himself, and sat upon the bed. 3. And Jacob said unto J oseph, God Almighty appeared unto me at Luz in the land of Canaan, and blessed me, 4. and said unto me, Behold, I will make thee fruitful, and multiply thee, and I will make of thee a multitude of people; and will give this land to thy seed after thee for an everlasting possession. 5. And now thy two sons, Ephraim and Manasseh, which were born unto thee in the land of Egypt before I came unto thee into Egypt, are mine; as Reuben and Simeon, they shall be mine. 6. And thy issue, which thou begettest after them, shall be thine, and shall be called after the name of their brethren in their inheritance. 7. And as for me, when I came from Padan, Rachel died by me in the land of Canaan in the way, when yet there was but a little way to come unto Ephrath: and I buried her there in the way of Ephrath; the same is Beth-lehem. 8. And Israel beheld Joseph's sons, and said, Who are these? 9. And Joseph said unto his father. They are my sons, whom God hath given me in this place. And he said, Bring them, I pray thee, unto me, and I will bless them. 10. Now the eyes of Israel were dim for age, so that he could not see. And he brought them near unto him; and he kissed them, and embraced them. 11. And Israel said unto Joseph, I had not thought to see thy face: and lo, God hath shewed

5. **are mine**, *i.e.* he adopted them as his own sons.

6. **shall be called**, etc., *i.e.* they shall be looked upon as part of Ephraim and Manasseh.

7. **by me**. Better, "to my sorrow."

me also thy seed. 12. And Joseph brought them out from between his knees, and he bowed himself with his face to the earth. 13. And Joseph took them both, Ephraim in his right hand toward Israel's left hand, and Manasseh in his left hand toward Israel's right hand, and brought them near unto him. 14. And Israel stretched out his right hand, and laid it upon Ephraim's head, who was the younger, and his left hand upon Manasseh's head, guiding his hands wittingly; for Manasseh was the firstborn.

15. And he blessed Joseph, and said, God, before whom my fathers Abraham and Isaac did walk, the God which fed me all my life long unto this day, 16. the Angel which redeemed me from all evil, bless the lads; and let my name be named on them, and the name of my fathers Abraham and Isaac; and let them grow into a multitude in the midst of the earth. 17. And when Joseph saw that his father laid his right hand upon the head of Ephraim, it displeased him: and he held up his father's hand, to remove it from Ephraim's head unto Manasseh's head. 18. And Joseph said unto his father, Not so, my father: for this is the firstborn; put thy right hand upon his head. 19. And his father refused, and said, I know it, my son, I know it: he also shall become a people, and he also shall be great: but truly his younger brother shall be greater than he, and his seed shall become a multitude of nations. 30. And he blessed them that day, saying, In thee shall Israel bless, saying, God make thee as Ephraim and as Manasseh: and he set Ephraim before Manasseh.

14. **guiding**, or "crossing."

19. **his younger brother**. The pre-eminence of the tribe of Ephraim was one of the chief obstacles in the way of national unity, *Cp.* Judg. 8, 12, and it was the jealousy between Ephraim and Judah that caused the disruption of the kingdom after Solomon's death.

21. And Israel said unto Joseph, Behold, I die: but God shall be with you, and bring you again unto the land of your fathers. 22. Moreover I have given to thee one portion above thy brethren, which I took out of the hand of the Amorite with my sword and with my bow.

Jacob blesses his sons—48:1. And Jacob called unto his sons, and said, Gather yourselves together, that I may tell you that which shall befall you in the last days.

2. Gather yourselves together, and hear, ye sons of Jacob; and hearken unto Israel your father.

3. Reuben, thou art my firstborn, my might, and the beginning of my strength, the excellency of dignity, and the excellency of power:

22. **portion**. R.V. marg., "mountain slope, Heb. *shechem*, shoulder." This is a play on the word Shechem, which lay between Ebal and Gerizim, thus occupying a commanding position in the country.

1. **the last days**, i.e. in the far future; the actual reference is to a time when the tribes of Israel were settled in Palestine, each with its well-defined character.

2-27. The following are the chief differences of rendering in the R.V.:

A.V.	R.V.
5. instruments of cruelty are in their habitations	weapons of violence are their swords,
6. secret	council.
digged down a wall	houghed an ox.
9. old lion-	lioness.
10. a lawgiver	the ruler's staff.
the gathering of the people be	the obedience of the peoples be.
14. two burdens	the sheepfolds.
15. that rest was good	a resting-place that it was good.
tribute	taskwork.
19. overcome	press upon.
overcome at the last	press upon their heel.
23. hated	persecuted

4. Unstable as water, thou shalt not excel.

5. Simeon and Levi are brethren; instruments of cruelty are in their habitations.

6. O my soul, come not thou into their secret; unto their assembly, mine honor, be not thou united: for in their anger they slew a man, and in their selfwill they digged down a wall.

7. Cursed be their anger, for it was fierce; and their wrath, for it was cruel: I will divide them in Jacob, and scatter them in Israel.

8. Judah, thou art he whom thy brethren shall praise: thy hand shall be in the neck of thine enemies; thy father's children shall bow down before thee.

9. Judah is a lion's whelp: from the prey, my son, thou art gone up: he stooped down, he couched as a lion, and as an old lion; who shall rouse him up?

10. The sceptre shall not depart from Judah, nor a lawgiver from between his feet, until Shiloh come; and unto him shall the gathering of the people be.

11. Binding his foal unto the vine, and his ass's colt unto the choice vine; he washed his garments in wine, and his clothes in the blood of grapes:

12. His eyes shall be red with wine, and his teeth white with milk.

7. **divide**. Simeon practically disappeared very early: Levi was scattered amongst various cities.

10. Both the text and the meaning of this verse are very doubtful. (1) The A.V. translation interprets **Shiloh** as a title of the future Messiah. This is certainly wrong. (2) The Septuagint reads, "till the things reserved for him come," or "until he come whose it is." (See Driver, p. 385, and Hastings' *D.B.* 4. p. 500.)

11, 12. These two verses are a picture of the peaceful land of Judah, a land of vineyards and rich pasturage.

13. Zebulun shall dwell at the haven of the sea; and he shall be for an haven of ships; and his border shall be unto Zidon.

14. Issachar is a strong ass couching down between two burdens:

15. And he saw that rest was good, and the land that it was pleasant; and bowed his shoulder to bear, and became a servant unto tribute.

16. Dan shall judge his people, as one of the tribes of Israel.

17. Dan shall be a serpent by the way, an adder in the path, that biteth the horse heels, so that his rider shall fall backward.

18. I have waited for thy salvation, O Lord.

19. Gad, a troop shall overcome him: but he shall overcome at the last.

20. Out of Asher his bread shall be fat, and he shall yield royal dainties.

21. Naphtali is a hind let loose: he giveth goodly words.

22. Joseph is a fruitful bough, even a fruitful bough by a well; whose branches run over the wall:

23. The archers have sorely grieved him, and shot at him, and hated him:

24. But his bow abode in strength, and the arms of his hands were made strong by the hands of the mighty

---

13. **Zebulun** may have touched the sea at one time near Mount Carmel, but, as far as we know it, it was entirely surrounded by Asher, Manasseh, Issachar, and Naphtali.

15. Issachar became subject to the Canaanites.

17. This is not a reproach; it is a wish.

adder, or "horned snake." The Cerastes cornutus is poisonous, and this verse accurately describes its habits.

19. **troop** = "a marauding band."

21. **goodly words**. See Judg. 5:1; Barak was of the tribe of Naphtali.

God of Jacob; (from thence is the shepherd, the stone of Israel:)

25. Even by the God of thy father, who shall help thee; and by the Almighty, who shall bless thee with blessings of heaven above, blessings of the deep that lieth under, blessings of the breasts, and of the womb:

26. The blessings of thy father have prevailed above the blessings of my progenitors unto the utmost bound of the everlasting hills: they shall be on the head of Joseph, and on the crown of the head of him that was separate from his brethren.

27. Benjamin shall ravin as a wolf: in the morning he shall devour the prey, and at night he shah divide the spoil. The death of Jacob—28. All these are the twelve tribes of Israel: and this is it that their father spake unto them, and blessed them; every one according to his blessing he blessed them. 29. And he charged them, and said unto them, I am to be gathered unto my people: bury me with my fathers in the cave that is in the field of Ephron

24. **from thence . . . Israel**, an obscure passage: as it stands it seems to mean either (1) "from God comes Joseph, Israel's shepherd, Israel's rock" or (2), omitting brackets, "his arms were made strong from thence, i.e. the heavens, even by the Shepherd, the Rock of Israel."

26. **The blessings . . . hills**. Rather, "the blessings of thy father [Jacob] ex ceed the blessings of the ancient mountains, the desirable things of the everlasting hills." This rendering means that the inherited blessings of the house of Joseph transcend all earthly advantages.

was separate from. Better, "is prince among."

Notes on Jacob's blessing upon his Family

i. The blessing of Jacob upon Ephraim and Manasseh in ch. 48 is in prose: it predicts the superiority of the descendants of Ephraim, the younger son of Joseph, over those of Manasseh, the elder. Joseph was to be represented among the tribes by his two sons.

ii. The blessing upon the sons of Jacob in ch. 49. is a poem, clearly written by one who knew the character of the tribes at a later day, and only pictorially ascribed to Jacob. (*Cp* . Deut. 33.

the Hittite, 30. in the cave that is in the field of Mach-pelah, which is before Mamre, in the land of Canaan, which Abraham bought with the field of Ephron the Hittite for a possession of a burying place. 31. There they buried Abraham and Sarah his wife; there they buried Isaac and Rebekah his wife; and there I buried Leah. 32. The purchase of the field and of the cave that is therein was from the children of Heth. 33. And when Jacob had made an end of commanding his sons, he gathered up his feet into the bed, and yielded up the ghost, and was gathered unto his people.

1. 1. And Joseph fell upon his father's face, and wept upon him, and kissed him. 2. And Joseph commanded his servants the physicians to embalm his father: and the physicians embalmed Israel. 3. And forty days were fulfilled for him; for so are fulfilled the days of those which are embalmed: and the Egyptians mourned for him threescore and ten days.

The burial of Jacob in Canaan—4. And when the days of his mourning were past, Joseph spake unto the house of Pharaoh, saying, If now I have found grace in your eyes, speak, I pray you, in the ears of Pharaoh, saying,

and Judges 5) The following points in this historical characterisation are to be noted:

1. Reuben: moral instability.
2, 3. Simeon and Levi: lawless violence.
4. Judah: power.
5. Zebulun: geographical position.
6. Issachar: slothfulness and lack of spirit.
7. Dan: cunning (regarded with approval).
8. Gad: warlike spirit.
9. Asher: fruitfulness of the land.
10. Naphtali: vigour, inspiration (?).
11. Joseph: fruitfulness, prosperity and power (= Ephraim and
    Manasseh).
12. Benjamin: warlike spirit.

5. My father made me swear, saying, Lo, I die: in my grave which I have digged for me in the land of Canaan, there shalt thou bury me. Now therefore let me go up, I pray thee, and bury my father, and I will come again. 6. And Pharaoh said, Go up, and bury thy father, according as he made thee swear. 7. And Joseph went up to bury his father: and with him went up all the servants of Pharaoh, the elders of his house, and all the elders of the land of Egypt, 8. and all the house of Joseph, and his brethren, and his father's house: only their little ones, and their flocks, and their herds, they left in the land of Goshen. 9. And there went up with him both chariots and horsemen: and it was a very great company. 10. And they came to the threshing floor of Atad, which is beyond Jordan, and there they mourned with a great and very sore lamentation: and he made a mourning for his father seven days. 11. And when the inhabitants of the land, the Canaanites, saw the mourning in the floor of Atad, they said, This is a grievous mourning to the Egyptians: wherefore the name of it was called Abel-mizraim, which is beyond Jordan. 12. And his sons did unto him according as he commanded them: 13. for his sons carried him into the land of Canaan, and buried him in the cave of the field of Machpelah, which Abraham bought with the field for a possession of a burying place of Ephron the Hittite, before Mamre. 14. And Joseph returned into Egypt, he, and his brethren, and all that went up with him to bury his father, after he had buried his father.

11. **mourning**, Heb. *ebel*. **Abel-mizraim**, contains the usual play on words: *abel* means "meadow," *mizraim* "of Egypt."

The complete reconciliation of Joseph and his brethren—15. And when Joseph's brethren saw that their father was dead, they said, Joseph will peradventure hate us, and will certainly requite us all the evil which we did unto him. 16. And they sent a messenger unto Joseph, saying, Thy father did command before he died, saying, 17. So shall ye say unto Joseph, Forgive, I pray thee now, the trespass of thy brethren, and their sin; for they did unto thee evil: and now, we pray thee, forgive the trespass of the servants of the God of thy father. And Joseph wept when they spake unto him. 18. And his brethren also went and fell down before his face; and they said, Behold, we be thy servants. 19. And Joseph said unto them, Fear not: for am I in the place of God? 20. But as for you, ye thought evil against me; but God meant it unto good, to bring to pass, as it is this day, to save much people alive. 21. Now therefore fear ye not: I will nourish you, and your little ones. And he comforted them, and spake kindly unto them.

The death of Joseph in Egypt—22. And Joseph dwelt in Egypt, he, and his father's house: and Joseph lived an hundred and ten years. 23. And Joseph saw Ephraim's children of the third generation: the children also of Machir the son of Manasseh were brought up upon Joseph's knees. 24. And Joseph said unto his brethren, I die: and God will surely visit you, and bring you out of this land unto the land which he sware to Abraham, to Isaac, and to Jacob. 25. And Joseph took an oath of the children of Israel, saying, God will surely visit you, and ye shall carry up my bones from hence. 26. So Joseph died, being an hundred and ten years old: and they embalmed him, and he was put in a coffin in Egypt.

PART III

ISRAEL IN EGYPT; AND THE EXODUS

EXODUS

NAME—The name of the second book of the Pentateuch signifies "going out" (Greek, *exodus*), and refers to the departure of the Israelites from Egypt.

Contents—It may be analysed briefly as follows:

I. Israel in Egypt.

II. The Exodus.

III. Israel on Sinai.

    (a) The Decalogue and the book of the Covenant.

    (b) The ratifying of the Covenant.

    (c) The Tabernacle.

Chronology—The Pharaoh of the Oppression was probably Ramses II. (*c*. 1300-1234 B.C., *Petrie*: *Cp*. Ex. 1:8). He was succeeded by Merenptah (or, Menephtah), in whose reign the Exodus occurred, about 1214 B.C. In Ex. 1:11 it is mentioned that the Israelites built by forced labor two store cities, Pithom and Raamses: of these the former has been identified with Pi-Tum; excavation has shown the existence of store chambers, and inscriptions prove that Ramses II was the founder of the city.

MOSES

Life—The greater part of the life of Moses belongs to the second volume of this series. The following is an outline of his life up to the crossing of the Red Sea.

A. First period: in Egypt.
  1. Birth and exposure.
  2. Rescue by Pharaoh's daughter, who brings him up.
  3. When grown up, slays the Egyptian taskmaster and
     flees to Midian.
B. Second period: in Midian.
  1. Marries Zipporah, daughter of Jethro.
  2. The revelation on Horeb: Moses has his mission
     imposed on him.
C. Third period: the Ten Plagues and the Exodus.

Comments on the narrative—The sources of the narrative are threefold, corresponding to the Jehovistic, Elohistic, and Priestly collections to which reference has already been made (see p. xiii). The only serious result of a division on these lines is to throw some doubt upon Aaron and the part he played in the events related. The figure of Moses himself is eminently historical.

In the earlier part of his life with which we are now dealing, the three chief features are (1) the revelation on Mount Horeb; (2) the Ten Plagues; (3) the Passover. Separate notes on these three subjects will be found in their proper place in the Biblical narrative.

ISRAEL IN EGYPT

Exodus 1-4

The family of Jacob—1:1. Now these are the names of the children of Israel, which came into Egypt; every man and his household came with Jacob. 2. Reuben, Simeon, Levi, and Judah, 3. Issachar, Zebulun, and Benjamin, 4. Dan, and Naphtali, Gad, and

Asher. 5. And all the souls that came out of the loins of Jacob were seventy souls: for Joseph was in Egypt already. 6. And Joseph died, and all his brethren, and all that generation. The oppression of Israel—7. And the children of Israel were fruitful, and increased abundantly, and multiplied, and waxed exceeding mighty; and the land was filled with them. 8. Now there arose up a new king over Egypt, which knew not Joseph. 9. And he said unto his people, Behold, the people of the children of Israel are more and mightier than we: 10. come on, let us deal wisely with them; lest they multiply, and it come to pass that, when there falleth out any war, they join also unto our enemies, and fight against us, and so get them up out of the land. 11. Therefore they did set over them taskmasters to afflict them with their burdens. And they built for Pharaoh treasure cities, Pithom and Raamses. 12. But the more they afflicted them, the more they multiplied and grew. And they were grieved because of the children of Israel. 13. And the Egyptians made the children of Israel to serve with rigor: 14. and they made their lives bitter with hard bondage, in mortar, and in brick, and in all manner of service in the field: all their service, wherein they made them serve, was with rigor.

The order to destroy the male children at birth—15. And the king of Egypt spake to the Hebrew midwives, of which the name of the one was Shiphrah, and the name of the other Puah: 16. and he said. When ye do the

8. **a new king**. Ramses II., *c.* 1300-1234 B.C.

11. **taskmasters**. Forced labor has always been the curse of Egypt down to the most modern times: see Modern Egypt, by Lord Cromer, ch. 1. It was the forced labor in Solomon's reign that was largely the cause of the disruption of the kingdom.

treasure cities. R.V. "store cities" See above, p. 143.

office of a midwife to the Hebrew women; if it be a son, then ye shall kill him: but if it be a daughter, then she shall live. 17. But the midwives feared God, and did not as the king of Egypt commanded them, but saved the men children alive. 18. And the king of Egypt called for the midwives, and said unto them, Why have ye done this thing, and have saved the men children alive? 19. And the midwives said unto Pharaoh, Because the Hebrew women are not as the Egyptian women; for they are delivered ere the midwives come in unto them. 20. Therefore God dealt well with the midwives: and the people multiplied, and waxed very mighty. 21. And it came to pass, because the midwives feared God, that he made them houses. 22. And Pharaoh charged all his people, saying, Every son that is born ye shall cast into the river, and every daughter ye shall save alive.

21. **he made them houses**, *i.e.* God granted that they should themselves become mothers and founders of families.

22. **the river**, *i.e.* the Nile.

1. According to Num. 26:59, the father of Moses was Amram, son of Kohath the Levite, and his mother was Jochebed, also a Levite. The family consisted of Aaron, Moses, and Miriam. This may be shown clearly thus:

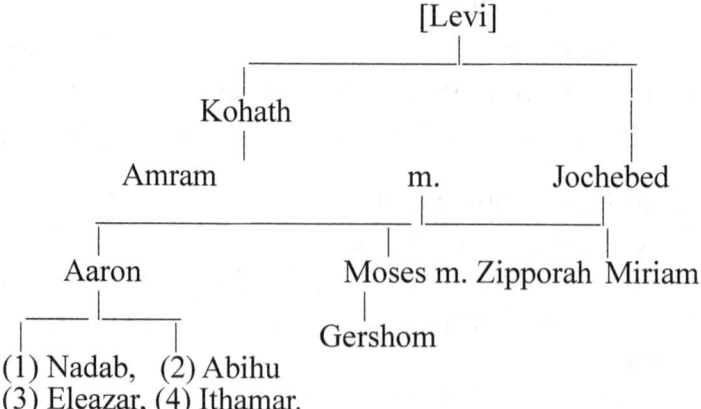

The birth and saving of Moses—2:1. And there went a man of the house of Levi, and took to wife a daughterof Levi. 2. And the woman conceived, and bare a son: and when she saw him that he was a goodly child, she hid him three months. 3. And when she could not longer hide him, she took for him an ark of bulrushes, and daubed it with slime and with pitch, and put the child therein; and she laid it in the flags by the river's brink. 4. And his sister stood afar off, to wit what would be done to him.

5. And the daughter of Pharaoh came down to wash herself at the river; and her maidens walked along by the river's side; and when she saw the ark among the flags, she sent her maid to fetch it. 6. And when she had opened it, she saw the child: and, behold, the babe wept. And she had compassion on him, and said, This is one of the Hebrews' children. 7. Then said his sister to Pharaoh's daughter, Shall I go and call to thee a nurse of the Hebrew women, that she may nurse the child for thee? 8. And Pharaoh's daughter said to her, Go. And the maid went and called the child's mother, 9. and Pharaoh's daughter said unto her, Take this child away, and nurse it for me, and I will give thee thy wages. And the woman took the child, and nursed it. 10. And the child grew, and she brought him unto Pharaoh's daughter, and he became her son. And she called his name Moses: and she said, Because I drew him out of the water.

2. **a goodly child**. *Cp*. Acts 7:20, Heb. 11:23.

3. **ark**, The same word in Hebrew is used for Noah's ark, a different word for the Ark carried by the Israelites in their wanderings.

bulrushes, *i.e.* papyrus, a reed used for making paper, boats, cloth, and many other things.

slime, *i.e.* bitumen, a kind of pitch.

flags, *i.e.* reeds.

10. **Moses ... drew**. Heb. *mosheh ... mashah*, to draw out. There is the usual play on words; the correct etymological derivation is uncertain.

Moses flees to Midian: he marries Zipporah—11. And it came to pass in those days, when Moses was grown, that he went out unto his brethren, and looked on their burdens: and he spied an Egyptian smiting an Hebrew, one of his brethren. 12. And he looked this way and that way, and when he saw that there was no man, he slew the Egyptian, and hid him in the sand. 13. And when he went out the second day, behold, two men of the Hebrews strove together: and he said to him that did the wrong. Wherefore smitest thou thy fellow? 14. And he said, Who made thee a prince and a judge over us? intendest thou to kill me, as thou killedst the Egyptian? And Moses feared, and said, Surely this thing is known. 15. Now when Pharaoh heard this thing, he sought to slay Moses. But Moses fled from the face of Pharaoh, and dwelt in the land of Midian: and he sat down by a well. 16. Now the priest of Midian had seven daughters: and they came and drew water, and filled the troughs to water their father's flock. 17. And the shepherds came and drove them away: but Moses stood up and helped them, and watered their flock. 18. And when they came to Reuel their father, he said, How is it that ye are come so soon today? 19. And they said, An Egyptian delivered us out of the hand of the shepherds, and also drew water enough for us, and watered the flock. 20. And he said unto his daughters, And where is he? why is it that ye have left the man? call him, that he may eat bread. 21. And Moses was content to dwell with the man: and he gave Moses Zipporah his daughter. 22. And she bare him a son, and he called his name Gershom: for he said, I have been a stranger in a strange land.

18. **Reuel**. Probably their grandfather. The father of Zippdrah is elsewhere called either Jethro or Hobab: in Num. 10:29 Hobab is the son of Reuel (A.V. "Raguel"); probably a mistake has been made in the present passage.

God hears the cries of Israel—23. And it came to pass in process of time, that the king of Egypt died: and the children of Israel sighed by reason of the bondage, and they cried, and their cry came up unto God by reason of the bondage. 24. And God heard their groaning, and God remembered his covenant with Abraham, with Isaac, and with Jacob. 25. And God looked upon the children of Israel, and God had respect unto them.

THE REVELATION OF MOUNT HOREB

The scene—The traditional view has been that Mount Sinai lay in the south of the Sinaitic peninsula, between the Gulf of Suez and the Gulf of Akaba, and Horeb and Sinai have been treated as alternative names for the same district. But, according to the latest theory Sinai, was a mountain near Kadesh Barnea, about 70 miles northwest of the Gulf of Akaba; and Mount Horeb, in Midian, was in the Arabian peninsula, east of the Red Sea, somewhere south-east of the Gulf of Akaba. There is no doubt, however, that the two names are confused in the Biblical narrative: the prophecy in Ex. 3:12, "Ye shall serve God upon this mountain," which refers to Horeb (verse 1), must be fulfilled by the encampment at Mt. Sinai (ch. 19. *Seq.*).

The revelation—The purpose of the Divine communication was twofold: (1) to impose on Moses his mission, viz. the deliverance of Israel; (2) to reveal God more fully to the understanding of men. Thus the passage about "the Bush "has a double importance—as a crisis in the history both of Israel and the whole world.

22. **Gershom**, the first syllable, ger = a sojourner.

The name Jehovah, or Yahweh, if not actually new, became henceforth quickened with a new significance. The actual derivative meaning of the word is obscure, but scholars agree in supposing that it suggests future development and progressive revelation by God of Himself to man: *"I will be what I will be."*

Moses on Mount Horeb: the Burning Bush—3:1. Now Moses kept the flock of Jethro his father-in-law, the priest of Midian: and he led the flock to the backside of the desert, and came to the mountain of God, even to Horeb. 2. And the angel of the Lord appeared unto him in a flame of fire out of the midst of a bush: and he looked, and, behold, the bush burned with fire, and the bush was not consumed. 3. And Moses said, I will now turn aside, and see this great sight, why the bush is not burnt. 4. And when the Lord saw that he turned aside to see, God called unto him out of the midst of the bush, and said, Moses, Moses. And he said, Here am I. 5. And he said, Draw not nigh hither: put off thy shoes from off thy feet, for the place whereon thou standest is holy ground. 6 . Moreover he said, I am the God of thy father, the God of Abraham, the God of Isaac, and the God of Jacob. And Moses hid his face; for he was afraid to look upon God.

God reveals His purpose and imposes on Moses his mission—7. And the Lord said, I have surely seen the affliction of my people which are in Egypt, and have heard their cry by reason of their taskmasters; for I know their

1. **the backside of the desert**, *i.e.* west: see on Gen. 14:15. This would mean near the coast, east of the Gulf of Akaba, according to the view which distinguishes Horeb from Sinai: but see p. 149.

5. **shoes**, *i.e.* sandals.

6. *Cp.* Mark 12:26, Luke 20:37.

sorrows; 8. and I am come down to deliver them out of the hand of the Egyptians, and to bring them up out of that land unto a good land and a large, unto a land flowing with milk and honey; unto the place of the Canaanites, and the Hittites, and the Amorites, and the Perizzites, and the Hivites, and the Jebusites. 9. Now therefore, behold, the cry of the children of Israel is come unto me: and I have also seen the oppression wherewith the Egyptians oppress them. 10. Come now therefore, and I will send thee unto Pharaoh, that thou mayest bring forth my people the children of Israel out of Egypt.

Revelation of the Name Jehovah—11. And Moses said unto God, Who am I, that I should go unto Pharaoh, and that I should bring forth the children of Israel out of Egypt? 12. And he said, Certainly I will be with thee; and this shall be a token unto thee, that I have sent thee: When thou hast brought forth the people out of Egypt, ye shall serve God upon this mountain. 13. And Moses said unto God, Behold, when I come unto the children of Israel, and shall say unto them, The God of your fathers hath sent me unto you; and they shall say to me, What is his name? what shall I say unto them? 14. And God said unto Moses, I AM THAT I AM: and he said, Thus shalt thou say unto the children of Israel, I AM hath sent me unto you. 15. And God said moreover unto Moses, Thus shalt thou say unto the children of Israel, The Lord God of your fathers, the God of Abraham,

12. **ye shall serve**, etc. See ch. 19 *seq.*, and remarks on p. 149. Horeb here obviously is equivalent to Sinai.

14. I am, etc. Best translated, I WILL BE THAT I WILL BE.

I AM hath sent me. Better, I WILL BE: Heb. *Ehyeh.*

15. The LORD God. R.V. "the Lord, the God." The Heb. *Jehovah* comes from the same root as *Ehyeh.* See verses 14, 18.

the God of Isaac, and the God of Jacob, hath sent me unto you: this is my name for ever, and this is my memorial unto all generations. 16. Go, and gather the elders of Israel together, and say unto them, The Lord God of your fathers, the God of Abraham, of Isaac, and of Jacob, appeared unto me, saying, I have surely visited you, and seen that which is done to you in Egypt: 17. and I have said, I will bring you up out of the affliction of Egypt unto the land of the Canaanites, and the Hittites, and the Amorites, and the Perizzites, and the Hivites, and the Jebusites, unto a land flowing with milk and honey. 18. And they shall hearken to thy voice: and thou shalt come, thou and the elders of Israel, unto the king of Egypt, and ye shall say unto him, The Lord God of the Hebrews hath met with us: and now let us go, we beseech thee, three days' journey into the wilderness, that we may sacrifice to the Lord our God. 19. And I am sure that the king of Egypt will not let you go, no, not by a mighty hand. 20. And I will stretch out my hand, and smite Egypt with all my wonders which I will do in the midst thereof: and after that he will let you go. 21. And I will give this people favor in the sight of the Egyptians: and it shall come to pass, that, when ye go, ye shall not go empty: 22. but every woman shall borrow of her neighbor, and of her that sojourneth in her house, jewels of silver, and jewels of gold, and raiment: and ye shall put them upon your sons, and upon your daughters; and ye shall spoil the Egyptians.

18. **The Lord, the God of the Hebrews** (R.V.). The popular conception of Jehovah at first was as a national God: that He was the only and universal God was revealed to the great teachers and prophets from Moses onwards, but did not meet with complete acceptance till as late as the Captivity. Belief in a national deity is known as monolatry, or henotheism, as opposed to monotheism.

19. not by a mighty hand, seems to mean "in spite of great acts which ought to convince him."

Moses faith strengthened by signs—4:1. And Moses answered and said, But, behold, they will not believe me, nor hearken unto my voice: for they will say, The Lord hath not appeared unto thee. 2. And the Lord said unto him, What is that in thine hand? And he said, A rod. 3. And he said, Cast it on the ground. And he cast it on the ground, and it became a serpent; and Moses fled from before it. 4. And the Lord said unto Moses, Put forth thine hand, and take it by the tail. And he put forth his hand, and caught it, and it became a rod in his hand: 5. That they may believe that the Lord God of their fathers, the God of Abraham, the God of Isaac, and the God of Jacob, hath appeared unto thee. 6. And the Lord said furthermore unto him, Put now thine hand into thy bosom. And he put his hand into his bosom: and when he took it out, behold, his hand was leprous as snow. 7. And he said, Put thine hand into thy bosom again. And he put his hand into his bosom again; and plucked it out of his bosom, and, behold, it was turned again as his other flesh. 8. And it shall come to pass, if they will not believe thee, neither hearken to the voice of the first sign, that they will believe the voice of the latter sign. 9. And it shall come to pass, if they will not believe also these two signs, neither hearken unto thy voice, that thou shalt take of the water of the river, and pour it upon the dry land: and the water which thou takest out of the river shall become blood upon the dry land.

Aaron appointed to help him—10. And Moses said unto the Lord. O my Lord, I am not eloquent, neither heretofore, nor

4. **And he put forth**, etc. in parenthesis: so too, in verse 7, "and he put forth his hand," etc.

since thou hast spoken unto thy servant: but I am slow of speech, and of a slow tongue, 11. And the Lord said unto him, Who hath made man's mouth? or who maketh the dumb, or deaf, or the seeing, or the blind? have not I the Lord? 12. Now therefore go, and I will be with thy mouth, and teach thee what thou shalt say. 13. And he said, O my Lord, send, I pray thee, by the hand of him whom thou wilt send. 14. And the anger of the Lord was kindled against Moses, and he said, Is not Aaron the Levite thy brother? I know that he can speak well. And also, behold, he cometh forth to meet thee: and when he seeth thee, he will be glad in his heart. 15. And thou shalt speak unto him, and put words in his mouth: and I will be with thy mouth, and with his mouth, and will teach you what ye shall do. 16. And he shall be thy spokesman unto the people: and he shall be, even he shall be to thee instead of a mouth, and thou shalt be to him instead of God. 17. And thou shalt take this rod in thine hand, wherewith thou shalt do signs.

Moses returns to Egypt—18. And Moses went and returned to Jethro his father in law, and said unto him, Let me go, I pray thee, and return unto my brethren which are in Egypt, and see whether they be yet alive. And Jethro said to Moses, Go in peace. 19. And the Lord said unto Moses in Midian, Go, return into Egypt: for all the men are dead which sought thy life. 20. And Moses

10. O Lord (R.V.). The names of God used in this volume correspond to the following Hebrew words: (1) Elohim, *Cp.* Gen. 1:1; (2) *El Shaddai*, God Almighty, *Cp.* Gen. 17:1; (3) *Jehovah*, or *Yahweh* (English Versions, the Lord), the national title from the time of Moses; (4) *Adhonai* (Lord), used also of men (Gen. 43:20).

13. **send, I pray thee**, etc., *i.e.* send some other messenger.

took his wife and his sons, and set them upon an ass, and he returned to the land of Egypt: and Moses took the rod of God in his hand. 21. And the Lord said unto Moses, When thou goest to return into Egypt, see that thou do all those wonders before Pharaoh, which I have put in thine hand: but I will harden his heart, that he shall not let the people go. 22. And thou shalt say unto Pharaoh. Thus saith the Lord, Israel is my son, even my firstborn: 23. and I say unto thee, Let my son go, that he may serve me: and if thou refuse to let him go, behold, I will slay thy son, even thy firstborn.

With Aaron he approaches the elders of Israel—27. And the Lord said to Aaron, Go into the wilderness to meet Moses. And he went, and met him in the mount of God, and kissed him. 28. And Moses told Aaron all the words of the Lord who had sent him, and all the signs which he had commanded him. 29. And Moses and Aaron went and gathered together all the elders of the children of Israel: 30. and Aaron spake all the words which the Lord had spoken unto Moses, and did the signs in the sight of the people. 31. And the people believed: and when they heard that the Lord had visited the children of Israel, and that he had looked upon their affliction, then they bowed their heads and worshipped.

He urges Pharaoh in vain to let the people go—v. 1. And afterward Moses and Aaron went in, and told Pharaoh, Thus saith the Lord God of Israel, Let my people go, that they may hold a feast unto me in the wilderness. 2. And Pharaoh said, Who is the Lord, that I should obey his voice to let Israel go? I know not the Lord, neither will I let Israel go. 3. And they said, The God of the Hebrews hath met with us: let us go, we pray thee, three days' journey into the desert, and sacrifice unto the Lord our God: lest he fall upon us with pestilence, or with the sword. 4. And the king of Egypt said unto them, Wherefore do ye, Moses and Aaron, let the people from their works? get you unto your burdens. 5. And Pharaoh said, Behold, the people of the land now are many, and ye make them rest from their burdens. 6. And Pharaoh commanded the same day the taskmasters of the people, and their officers, saying, 7. Ye shall no more give the people straw to make brick, as heretofore: let them go and gather straw for themselves. 8. And the tale of the bricks, which they did make heretofore, ye shall lay upon them; ye shall not diminish ought thereof: for they be idle; therefore they cry, saying, Let us go and sacrifice to our God. 9. Let there more work be laid upon the men, that they may labor therein; and let them not regard vain words.

The oppression of the Israelites becomes more cruel; their murmurings—10. And the taskmasters of the people went out, and their officers, and they spake to the people, saying, Thus saith Pharaoh, I will not give you straw. 11. Go ye, get you straw where ye can find it: yet not ought of your works shall be diminished. 12. So the people were scattered abroad throughout all the land of Egypt to gather stubble instead of straw. 13. And the taskmasters hasted them, saying, Fulfil your works, your daily tasks, as when there was straw. 14. And the officers of the children of Israel, which Pharaoh's taskmasters had set over them, were beaten, and demanded, Wherefore

4. **let** = hinder, stop.

7. **brick**. Unbaked bricks were made of Nile mud, mixed with chopped straw to act as a "binder."

8. **tale** = full number.

have ye not fulfilled your task in making brick both yesterday and to day, as heretofore? 15. Then the officers of the children of Israel came and cried unto Pharaoh, saying, Wherefore dealest thou thus with thy servants? 16. There is no straw given unto thy servants, and they say to us, Make brick: and, behold, thy servants are beaten; but the fault is in thine own people. 17. But he said, Ye are idle, ye are idle: therefore ye say, Let us go and do sacrifice to the Lord. 18. Go therefore now, and work; for there shall no straw be given you, yet shall ye deliver the tale of bricks. 19. And the officers of the children of Israel did see that they were in evil case, after it was said, Ye shall not minish ought from your bricks of your daily task.

20. And they met Moses and Aaron, who stood in the way, as they came forth from Pharaoh: 21. and they said unto them, The Lord look upon you, and judge; because ye have made our savour to be abhorred in the eyes of Pharaoh, and in the eyes of his servants, to put a sword in their hand to slay us. 22. And Moses returned unto the Lord, and said, Lord, wherefore hast thou so evil entreated this people? why is it that thou hast sent me? 23. For since I came to Pharaoh to speak in thy name, he hath done evil to this people; neither hast thou delivered thy people at all.

God renews His promise—6:1. Then the Lord said unto Moses, Now shalt thou see what I will do to Pharaoh: for with a strong hand shall he let them go, and with a strong hand shall he drive them out of his land. 2. And God spake unto Moses, and said unto him, I am the Lord:

1. **with a strong hand**, *i.e.* in consequence of the strong hand of Jehovah, as seen in the Ten Plagues.

3. and I appeared unto Abraham, unto Isaac, and unto Jacob, by the name of God Almighty, but by my name JEHOVAH was I not known to them. 4. And I have also established my covenant with them, to give them the land of Canaan, the land of their pilgrimage, wherein they were strangers. 5. And I have also heard the groaning of the children of Israel, whom the Egyptians keep in bondage; and I have remembered my covenant. 6. Wherefore say unto the children of Israel, I am the Lord, and I will bring you out from under the burdens of the Egyptians, and I will rid you out of their bondage, and I will redeem you with a stretched out arm, and with great judgments: 7. and I will take you to me for a people, and I will be to you a God: and ye shall know that I am the Lord your God, which bringeth you out from under the burdens of the Egyptians. 8. And I will bring you in unto the land, concerning the which I did swear to give it to Abraham, to Isaac, and to Jacob; and I will give it you for an heritage: I am the Lord.

9. And Moses spake so unto the children of Israel: but they hearkened not unto Moses for anguish of spirit, and for cruel bondage. 10. And the Lord spake unto Moses, saying, 11. Go in, speak unto Pharaoh king of Egypt, that he let the children of Israel go out of his land. 12. And Moses spake before the Lord, saying, Behold,

3. **JEHOVAH**. Vv. 2-12 are ascribed to the Priestly source. This supplies us with a simple explanation of the statement that the name Jehovah was not known in patriarchal times, viz. that the different narratives woven together in the Pentateuch, as we have it, do not agree on all points, because they are derived from different and independent sources.

6. **redeem**. Cp. 15:13. The idea of "redemption" pervades all Biblical thought, from Gen. 48:16, where Jacob speaks of "the angel which hath redeemed me from all evil," to Rev. v. 9, "thou hast redeemed us by thy blood."

the children of Israel have not hearkened unto me; how then shall Pharaoh hear me, who am of uncircumcised lips? 13. And the Lord spake unto Moses and unto Aaron, and gave them a charge unto the children of Israel, and unto Pharaoh king of Egypt, to bring the children of Israel out of the land of Egypt.

THE TEN PLAGUES

In the account of the Ten Plagues we may observe (a) the freedom from plague of the land of Goshen; (b) the impression produced on the minds of the Egyptians, who were forced to fear the power of Jehovah because Moses proved more than a match for their own magicians; (c) the nature of the plagues themselves: in these the miraculous element seems to have been the use by God of His own laws—the laws of nature—for a special purpose, namely, to terrify the Egyptians, and at the same time to convince and strengthen the people of Israel. Parallels to every plague can be quoted, and they are all closely connected with the natural condition of the country, *e.g.* local winds, Nile mud, and so forth.

1. Changing of the water into blood. The redness of the Nile water at certain times is due to the presence of minute organisms washed down the river after a great inundation. The Egyptians largely depended on fish for food.

2. Frogs. This plague can be illustrated by experience both in Egypt and in other parts of the world.

3 and 4. Lice and flies. The word "lice" seems to mean stinging fly or gnat. "Flies" represents a word of

12. **of uncircumcised lips**, *i.e.* who would be regarded by Pharaoh as unclean.

uncertain meaning; perhaps it should be simply "swarms of insects"

5 and 6. Murrain and boils. "In view of the recently discovered capacity of mosquitos and gnats to carry contagion, it is striking to note that disease of man and beast so quickly followed the swarms of flies." (Hastings, D.B.: "Plagues of Egypt.")

7. Hail.

8. Locusts. The plague of locusts is one familiar in Africa and other parts of the world today; for a description see Joel 1, 2.

9. Darkness. This was probably caused by a southwest wind called *hamsin*, which fills the atmosphere with a fine dust, and lasts about three days: see The Wisdom of Solomon, 17.

10. Death of the firstborn: the coincidence of plague and the *hamsin* has been noticed by man authorities.

The Ten Plagues
Exodus vii—xi

Preparations for the contest—7:1. And the Lord said unto Moses, See, I have made thee a god to Pharaoh: and Aaron thy brother shall be thy prophet. 2. Thou shalt speak all that I command thee: and Aaron thy brother shall speak unto Pharaoh, that he send the children of Israel out of his land. 3. And I will harden Pharaoh's heart, and multiply my signs and my wonders in the land of Egypt. 4. But Pharaoh shall not hearken unto you, that I may lay my hand upon Egypt, and bring forth mine armies, and my people the children of Israel, out of the

1. **prophet**, in the sense of "spokesman": so, in Æsch. *Eum.* 19, Apollo is called the "prophet," *i.e.* interpreter of the will, of Zeus.

land of Egypt by great judgments. 5. And the Egyptians shall know that I am the Lord, when I stretch forth mine hand upon Egypt, and bring out the children of Israel from among them. 6. And Moses and Aaron did as the Lord commanded them, so did they. 7. And Moses was fourscore years old, and Aaron fourscore and three years old, when they spake unto Pharaoh. 8. And the Lord spake unto Moses and unto Aaron, saying, 9. When Pharaoh shall speak unto you, saying, Shew a miracle for you: then thou shalt say unto Aaron, Take thy rod, and cast it before Pharaoh, and it shall become a serpent.

10. And Moses and Aaron went in unto Pharaoh, and they did so as the Lord had commanded: and Aaron cast down his rod before Pharaoh, and before his servants, and it became a serpent. 11. Then Pharaoh also called the wise men and the sorcerers: now the magicians of Egypt, they also did in like manner with their enchantments. 12. For they cast down every man his rod, and they became serpents: but Aaron's rod swallowed up their rods. 13. And he hardened Pharaoh's heart, that he hearkened not unto them; as the Lord had said.

(1) *The river turned into blood*—14. And the Lord said unto Moses, Pharaoh's heart is hardened, he refuseth to let the people go. 15. Get thee unto Pharaoh in the morning; lo, he goeth out unto the water; and thou shalt stand by the river's brink against he come; and the rod which was turned to a serpent shalt thou take in thine hand. 16. And thou shalt say unto him, The Lord God of the Hebrews hath sent me unto thee, saying, Let my

11. **magicians**. See Gen. 41:8; *Cp.* 2 Tim. 3:8. "The power possessed by a man who was skilled in the knowledge and working of magic was believed to be almost boundless" (Budge's *Egyptian Magic*, p. x).

people go, that they may serve me in the wilderness: and, behold, hitherto thou wouldest not hear. 17. Thus saith the Lord, In this thou shalt know that I am the Lord: behold, I will smite with the rod that is in mine hand upon the waters which are in the river, and they shall be turned to blood. 18. And the fish that is in the river shall die, and the river shall stink; and the Egyptians shall lothe to drink of the water of the river. 19. And the Lord spake unto Moses, Say unto Aaron, Take thy rod, and stretch out thine hand upon the waters of Egypt, upon their streams, upon their rivers, and upon their ponds, and upon all their pools of water, that they may become blood; and that there may be blood throughout all the land of Egypt, both in vessels of wood, and in vessels of stone. 20.   And Moses and Aaron did so, as the Lord commanded; and he lifted up the rod, and smote the waters that were in the river, in the sight of Pharaoh, and in the sight of his servants; and all the waters that were in the river were turned to blood. 21. And the fish that was in the river died; and the river stank, and the Egyptians could not drink of the water of the river; and there was blood throughout all the land of Egypt. 22. And the magicians of Egypt did so with their enchantments: and Pharaoh's heart was hardened, neither did he hearken unto them; as the Lord had said. 23. And Pharaoh turned and went into his house, neither did he set his heart to this also. 24. And all the Egyptians digged round about the river for water to drink; for they could

22. **And the magicians**, etc. This sentence may have been inserted from verse 11; for, according to the story, there was no water in Egypt unpolluted. Possibly the similar statement in 8:7 may be explained in the same way.

23. **set his heart to this** = lay this to heart.

not drink of the water of the river. 25. And seven days were fulfilled, after that the Lord had smitten the river.

(2) *The Frogs*—8:1. And the Lord spake unto Moses, Go unto Pharaoh, and say unto him, Thus saith the Lord, Let my people go, that they may serve me. 2. And if thou refuse to let them go, behold, I will smite all thy borders with frogs: 3. and the river shall bring forth frogs abundantly, which shall go up and come into thine house, and into thy bedchamber, and upon thy bed, and into the house of thy servants, and upon thy people, and into thine ovens, and into thy kneadingtroughs: 4. and the frogs shall come up both on thee, and upon thy people, and upon all thy servants. 5. And the Lord spake unto Moses, Say unto Aaron, Stretch forth thine hand with thy rod over the streams, over the rivers, and over the ponds, and cause frogs to come up upon the land of Egypt. 6. And Aaron stretched out his hand over the waters of Egypt; and the frogs came up, and covered the land of Egypt. 7. And the magicians did so with their enchantments, and brought up frogs upon the land of Egypt. 8. Then Pharaoh called for Moses and Aaron, and said, Intreat the Lord, that he may take away the frogs from me, and from my people; and I will let the people go, that they may do sacrifice unto the Lord. 9. And Moses said unto Pharaoh, Glory over me: when shall I intreat for thee, and for thy servants, and for thy people, to destroy the frogs from thee and thy houses, that they may remain in the river only? 10. And he said, To morrow. And he said, Be it according to thy

---

3. **ovens** = jars about 3 feet high, heated inside by burning wood or dried grass. (Matt. 6:30.)

9. **Glory over me seems to mean**, Command me to this extent.

word: that thou mayest know that there is none like unto the Lord our God. 11. And the frogs shall depart from thee, and from thy houses, and from thy servants, and from thy people; they shall remain in the river only. 12. And Moses and Aaron went out from Pharaoh: and Moses cried unto the Lord because of the frogs which he had brought against Pharaoh. 13. And the Lord did according to the word of Moses; and the frogs died out of the houses, out of the villages, and out of the fields. 14. And they gathered them together upon heaps: and the land stank. 15. But when Pharaoh saw that there was a respite, he hardened his heart, and hearkened not unto them; as the Lord had said.

(3) *The Lice*—16. And the Lord said unto Moses, Say unto Aaron, Stretch out thy rod, and smite the dust of the land, that it may become lice throughout all the land of Egypt. 17. And they did so; for Aaron stretched out his hand with his rod, and smote the dust of the earth, and it became lice in man, and in beast; all the dust of the land became lice throughout all the land of Egypt. 18. And the magicians did so with their enchantments to bring forth lice, but they could not: so there were lice upon man, and upon beast. 19. Then the magicians said unto Pharaoh, This is the finger of God: and Pharaoh's heart was hardened and he hearkened not unto them; as the Lord had said.

(4) *The Flies*—20. And the Lord said unto Moses, Rise up early in the morning, and stand before Pharaoh; lo, he cometh forth to the water; and say unto him, Thus saith the Lord, Let my people go, that they may serve me. 21. Else, if thou wilt not let my people go, behold, I will send swarms of flies upon thee, and upon thy servants, and upon thy people, and into thy houses: and the houses

of the Egyptians shall be full of swarms of flies, and also the ground whereon they are. 22. And I will sever in that day the land of Goshen, in which my people dwell, that no swarms of flies shall be there; to the end thou mayest know that I am the Lord in the midst of the earth. 23. And I will put a division between my people and thy people: to morrow shall this sign be. 24. And the Lord did so; and there came a grievous swarm of flies into the house of Pharaoh, and into his servants' houses, and into all the land of Egypt: the land was corrupted by reason of the swarm of flies.

25. And Pharaoh called for Moses and for Aaron, and said, Go ye, sacrifice to your God in the land. 26. And Moses said, It is not meet so to do; for we shall sacrifice the abomination of the Egyptians to the Lord our God: lo, shall we sacrifice the abomination of the Egyptians before their eyes, and will they not stone us? 27. We will go three days' journey into the wilderness, and sacrifice to the Lord our God, as he shall command us. 28. And Pharaoh said, I will let you go, that ye may sacrifice to the Lord your God in the wilderness; only ye shall not go very far away: intreat for me. 29. And Moses said. Behold, I go out from thee, and I will intreat the Lord that the swarms of flies may depart from Pharaoh, from his servants, and from his people, to morrow: but let not Pharaoh deal deceitfully any more in not letting the people go to sacrifice to the Lord. 30. And Moses went out from Pharaoh, and intreated the Lord. 31. And the Lord did according to the word of Moses; and he removed the swarms of flies from Pharaoh, from his servants, and from

26. **we shall**, *etc.* The meaning is: "Our sacrifices to Jehovah, requiring as they do the slaughter of animals held sacred in this country, will be an abomination to the Egyptians."

his people; there remained not one. 32. And Pharaoh hardened his heart at this time also, neither would he let the people go.

(5) *The murrain on beasts*—9:1. Then the Lord said unto Moses, Go in unto Pharaoh, and tell him, Thus saith the Lord God of the Hebrews, Let my people go, that they may serve me. 2. For if thou refuse to let them go, and wilt hold them still, 3. behold, the hand of the Lord is upon thy cattle which is in the field, upon the horses, upon the asses, upon the camels, upon the oxen, and upon the sheep: there shall be a very grievous murrain. 4. And the Lord shall sever between the cattle of Israel and the cattle of Egypt: and there shall nothing die of all that is the children's of Israel. 5. And the Lord appointed a set time, saying, To morrow the Lord shall do this thing in the land. 6. And the Lord did that thing on the morrow, and all the cattle of Egypt died: but of the cattle of the children of Israel died not one. 7. And Pharaoh sent, and, behold, there was not one of the cattle of the Israelites dead. And the heart of Pharaoh was hardened, and he did not let the people go.

(6) *The Boils*—8. And the Lord said unto Moses and unto Aaron, Take to you handfuls of ashes of the furnace, and let Moses sprinkle it toward the heaven in the sight of Pharaoh. 9. And it shall become small dust in all the land of Egypt, and shall be a boil breaking forth with blains upon man, and upon beast, throughout all the land of Egypt. 10. And they took ashes of the furnace, and stood before Pharaoh; and Moses sprinkled it up toward heaven; and it became a boil breaking forth with blains upon man, and upon beast. 11. And the magicians could not stand before Moses because of the boils; for the boil

was upon the magicians, and upon all the Egyptians. 12. And the Lord hardened the heart of Pharaoh, and he hearkened not unto them; as the Lord had spoken unto Moses. 13. And the Lord said unto Moses, Rise up early in the morning, and stand before Pharaoh, and say unto him, Thus saith the Lord God of the Hebrews, Let my people go, that they may serve me. 14. For I will at this time send all my plagues upon thine heart, and upon thy servants, and upon thy people; that thou mayest know that there is none like me in all the earth. 15. For now I will stretch out my hand, that I may smite thee and thy people with pestilence; and thou shalt be cut off from the earth. 16. And in very deed for this cause have I raised thee up, for to shew in thee my power; and that my name may be declared throughout all the earth. 17. As yet exaltest thou thyself against my people, that thou wilt not let them go? 18. Behold, tomorrow about this time I will cause it to rain a very grievous hail, such as hath not been in Egypt since the foundation thereof even until now. 19. Send therefore now, and gather thy cattle, and all that thou hast in the field; for upon every man and beast which shall be found in the field, and shall not be brought home, the hail shall come down upon them, and they shall die. 20. He that feared the word of the Lord among the servants of Pharaoh made his servants and his cattle flee into the houses: 21. and he that regarded not the word of the Lord left his servants and his cattle in the field.

(7) *The Hail*— 22. And the Lord said unto Moses,

16. **raised thee up**. R.V. "made thee to stand" *i.e.* to survive. The A.V. corresponds more closely to the form of the words quoted in Rom. 9:17, which see.

Stretch forth thine hand toward heaven, that there may be hail in all the land of Egypt, upon man, and upon beast, and upon every herb of the field, throughout the land of Egypt. 23. And Moses stretched forth his rod toward heaven: and the Lord sent thunder and hail, and the fire ran along upon the ground; and the Lord rained hail upon the land of Egypt. 24. So there was hail, and fire mingled with the hail, very grievous, such as there was none like it in all the land of Egypt since it became a nation. 25. And the hail smote throughout all the land of Egypt all that was in the field, both man and beast; and the hail smote every herb of the field, and brake every tree of the field. 26. Only in the land of Goshen, where the children of Israel were, was there no hail.

27. And Pharaoh sent, and called for Moses and Aaron, and said unto them, I have sinned this time: the Lord is righteous, and I and my people are wicked. 28. Intreat the Lord (for it is enough) that there be no more mighty thunderings and hail; and I will let you go, and ye shall stay no longer. 29. And Moses said unto him, As soon as I am gone out of the city, I will spread abroad my hands unto the Lord; and the thunder shall cease, neither shall there be any more hail; that thou mayest know how that the earth is the Lord's. 30. But as for thee and thy servants, I know that ye will not yet fear the Lord God. 31. And the flax and the barley was smitten: for the barley was in the ear, and the flax was boiled. 32. But the wheat and the rie were not smitten: for they

24. **mingled**. R.V. marg., "flashing continually amidst."

31, 32. The time of year would be February—March.

31. **boiled** means, had reached the pod stage, "was in bloom."

32. **rie**. R.V. "spelt." Described as "a hard, coarse, bearded wheat, much cultivated formerly for fodder." (*Murray's III. B.D.*).

were not grown tip. 33. And Moses went out of the city from Pharaoh, and spread abroad his hands unto the Lord: and the thunders and hail ceased, and the rain was not poured upon the earth. 34. And when Pharaoh saw that the rain and the hail and the thunders were ceased, he sinned yet more, and hardened his heart, he and his servants. 35. And the heart of Pharaoh was hardened, neither would he let the children of Israel go; as the Lord had spoken by Moses.

(8) *The Locusts*—10:1. And the Lord said unto Moses, Go in unto Pharaoh: for I have hardened his heart, and the heart of his servants, that I might shew these my signs before him: 2. and that thou mayest tell in the ears of thy son, and of thy son's son, what things I have wrought in Egypt, and my signs which I have done among them; that ye may know how that I am the Lord. 3. And Moses and Aaron came in unto Pharaoh, and said unto him, Thus saith the Lord God of the Hebrews, How long wilt thou refuse to humble thyself before me? let my people go, that they may serve me. 4. Else, if thou refuse to let my people go, behold, to morrow will I bring the locusts into thy coast: 5. and they shall cover the face of the earth, that one cannot be able to see the earth: and they shall eat the residue of that which is escaped, which remaineth unto you from the hail, and shall eat every tree which groweth for you out of the field: 6. and they shall fill thy houses, and the houses of all thy servants, and the houses of all the Egyptians; which neither thy fathers, nor thy fathers' fathers have seen, since the day that they were upon the earth unto this day. And he

2. **what . . . Egypt**: better, "how I have made a toy of the Egyptians" (McNeile).

turned himself, and went out from Pharaoh. 7. And Pharaoh's servants said unto him, How long shall this man be a snare unto us? let the men go, that they may serve the Lord their God: knowest thou not yet that Egypt is destroyed? 8. And Moses and Aaron were brought again unto Pharaoh: and he said unto them, Go, serve the Lord your God: but who are they that shall go? 9. And Moses said, We will go with our young and with our old, with our sons and with our daughters, with our flocks and with our herds will we go; for we must hold a feast unto the Lord. 10. And he said unto them, Let the Lord be so with you, as I will let you go, and your little ones: look to it; for evil is before you.
11. Not so: go now ye that are men, and serve the Lord; for that ye did desire. And they were driven out from Pharaoh's presence.

12. And the Lord said unto Moses, Stretch out thine hand over the land of Egypt for the locusts, that they may come up upon the land of Egypt, and eat every herb of the land, even all that the hail hath left. 13. And Moses stretched forth his rod over the land of Egypt, and the Lord brought an east wind upon the land all that day, and all that night; and when it was morning, the east wind brought the locusts. 14. And the locusts went up over all the land of Egypt, and rested in all the coasts of Egypt: very grievous were they; before them there were no such locusts as they, neither after them shall be such. 15. For they covered the face of the whole earth, so that the land was darkened; and they did eat every herb of the land, and

---

10. Paraphrase: "Your purpose is evil; look to your God for help, not to me: may He be as willing to help you as I am!"

all the fruit of the trees which the hail had left: and there remained not any green thing in the trees, or in the herbs of the field, through all the land of Egypt. 16. Then Pharaoh called for Moses and Aaron in haste; and he said, I have sinned against the Lord your God, and against you. 17. Now therefore forgive, I pray thee, my sin only this once, and intreat the Lord your God, that he may take away from me this death only. 18. And he went out from Pharaoh, and intreated the Lord. 19. And the Lord turned a mighty strong west wind, which took away the locusts, and cast them into the Red Sea; there remained not one locust in all the coasts of Egypt. 20. But the Lord hardened Pharaoh's heart, so that he would not let the children of Israel go.

(9) *The Darkness*—21. And the Lord said unto Moses, Stretch out thine hand toward heaven, that there may be darkness over the land of Egypt, even darkness which may be felt. 22. And Moses stretched forth his hand toward heaven; and there was a thick darkness in all the land of Egypt three days: 23. they saw not one another, neither rose any from his place for three days: but all the children of Israel had light in their dwellings. 24. And Pharaoh called unto Moses, and said, Go ye, serve the Lord; only let your flocks and your herds be stayed: let your little ones also go with you. 25. And Moses said, Thou must give us also sacrifices and burnt offerings, that we may sacrifice unto the Lord our God. 26. Our cattle also shall go with us; there shall not an hoof be left behind; for thereof must we take to serve the Lord our God; and we know not with what we must serve the Lord, until we come thither.

27. But the Lord hardened Pharaoh's heart, and he

would not let them go. 28. And Pharaoh said unto him, Get thee from me, take heed to thyself, see my face no more; for in that day thou seest my face thou shalt die. 29. And Moses said, Thou hast spoken well, I will see thy face again no more.

(10 a) *The Death of the Firstborn* (see 12:29, 30, p. 177)— 11:1. And the Lord said unto Moses, Yet will I bring one plague more upon Pharaoh, and upon Egypt; afterwards he will let you go hence: when he shall let you go, he shall surely thrust you out hence altogether. 2. Speak now in the ears of the people, and let every man borrow of his neighbor, and every woman of her neighbor, jewels of silver, and jewels of gold. 3. And the Lord gave the people favor in the sight of the Egyptians. Moreover the man Moses was very great in the land of Egypt, in the sight of Pharaoh's servants, and in the sight of the people. 4. And Moses said. Thus saith the Lord, About midnight will I go out into the midst of Egypt: 5. and all the firstborn in the land of Egypt shall die, from the firstborn of Pharaoh that sitteth upon his throne, even unto the firstborn of the maidservant that is behind the mill; and all the firstborn of beasts. 6. And there shall be a great cry throughout all the land of Egypt, such as there was none like it, nor shall be like it any more. 7. But against any of the children of Israel shall not a dog move his tongue, against man or beast: that ye may know how that the Lord doth put a difference between the Egyptians and Israel. 8. And all these thy servants shall come down unto me, and bow down themselves unto me, saying, Get thee out, and all the people that follow thee: and after that I will go out. And he went out from Pharaoh in a great anger. 9. And the Lord said unto Moses,

Pharaoh shall not hearken unto you; that my wonders may be multiplied in the land of Egypt. 10. And Moses and Aaron did all these wonders before Pharaoh: and the Lord hardened Pharaoh's heart, so that he would not let the children of Israel go out of his land.

THE PASSOVER

Two points in connection with the institution of the Passover seem to be clear: *first*, according to the writers of the books of the Old Testament, its historical origin was the occasion of the deliverance of Israel out of Egypt, when the firstborn of the Egyptians were slain, and the angel of death passed over the houses of the Israelites in Goshen; *secondly*, its celebration took place at a time of year which brought it into connection with a previously existing festival: thus it came to contain other ideas besides the commemoration of the redemption from Egypt. Its significance was many-sided, and may be summed up thus:

1. Historical: the Passover, or "passing over" of the angel.
2. Harvest festival: the Feast of Unleavened Bread (which was an alternative name of the Passover) was marked by the eating of *mazzoth*, or unleavened cakes, for seven days. These *mazzoth* recalled the bread made with the new corn at the beginning of the harvest. This was the earliest harvest festival of the year, and was older in origin than the Exodus.
3. Sacrifice of the firstborn, (*cf.* Gen. 4:2-4; Exod. 13:12.)
4. Piacular; *i.e.* to make atonement.

5. A blood covenant with the Deity, chiefly as a means of averting disease.

The chief details of the Passover are these:

Time: Abib 14-21 (later called Nisan), *i.e.* April.

Abib 14: eating of the Paschal[1] meal.

Ritual: Choice of the lamb without blemish.

Killing of the lamb.

Smearing the door with hyssop dipped in the blood.

Eating of the lamb with *mazzoth* and bitter herbs.

All to be prepared for a journey.

No stranger (*i.e.* uncircumcised person) present.

Only unleavened bread eaten for seven days.

To Christians the chief interest of the Passover is its connection with the institution of the Lord's Supper. This opens up the difficult question of reconciling the different accounts of the Supper contained in the Gospels; but here it is sufficient to say that "in the highest act of Christian worship all the main features in the Passover are taken up and receive their full and eternal significance" (McNeile, *Exodus*).

Institution of the Passover, and the Exodus
Exodus 12—15:21

Regulations for the Passover and Feast of Unleavened Bread—12:1. And the Lord spake unto Moses and Aaron in the land of Egypt, saying, 2. This month shall be unto you the beginning of months: it shall be the first month of the year to you.

---

[1] The word Paschal is derived, through the Greek, from the Hebrew *pasah*, to pass over.

2. **month**. The month Abib was regarded as the first month, because it was the season of the first ripe corn.

3. Speak ye unto all the congregation of Israel, saying, In the tenth day of this month they shall take to them every man a lamb, according to the house of their fathers, a lamb for an house: 4. and if the household be too little for the lamb, let him and his neighbor next unto his house take it according to the number of the souls; every man according to his eating shall make your count for the lamb. 5. Your lamb shall be without blemish, a male of the first year: ye shall take it out from the sheep, or from the goats: 6. and ye shall keep it up until the fourteenth day of the same month: and the whole assembly of the congregation of Israel shall kill it in the evening. 7. And they shall take of the blood, and strike it on the two side posts and on the upper door post of the houses, wherein they shall eat it. 8. And they shall eat the flesh in that night, roast with fire, and unleavened bread; and with bitter herbs they shall eat it. 9. Eat not of it raw, nor sodden at all with water, but roast with fire; his head with his legs, and with the purtenance thereof. 10. And ye shall let nothing of it remain until the morning; and that which remaineth of it until the morning ye shall burn with fire.

11. And thus shall ye eat it; with your loins girded, your shoes on your feet, and your staff in your hand; and ye shall eat it in haste: it is the Lord's passover. 12. For I will pass through the land of Egypt this night, and will smite all the firstborn in the land of Egypt, both man and beast; and against all the gods of Egypt I will execute judgment: I am the Lord. 13. And the blood shall be to you for a token upon the houses where ye are:

8. **bitter herbs**, *e.g.* wild lettuce and endive.
9. **sodden**, *i.e.* boiled.

and when I see the blood, I will pass over you, and the plague shall not be upon you to destroy you, when I smite the land of Egypt. 14. And this day shall be unto you for a memorial; and ye shall keep it a feast to the Lord throughout your generations; ye shall keep it a feast by an ordinance for ever. 15. Seven days shall ye eat unleavened bread; even the first day ye shall put away leaven out of your houses: for whosoever eateth leavened bread from the first day until the seventh day, that soul shall be cut off from Israel. 16. And in the first day there shall be an holy convocation, and in the seventh day there shall be an holy convocation to you; no manner of work shall be done in them, save that which every man must eat, that only may be done of you. 17. And ye shall observe the feast of unleavened bread; for in this selfsame day have I brought your armies out of the land of Egypt: therefore shall ye observe this day in your generations by an ordinance for ever.

18. In the first month, on the fourteenth day of the month at even, ye shall eat unleavened bread, until the one and twentieth day of the month at even. 19. Seven days shall there be no leaven found in your houses: for whosoever eateth that which is leavened, even that soul shall be cut off from the congregation of Israel, whether he be a stranger, or born in the land. 20. Ye shall eat nothing leavened; in all your habitations shall ye eat unleavened bread.

21. Then Moses called for all the elders of Israel, and said unto them, Draw out and take you a lamb according

19. leaven, which causes fermentation, was therefore associated with the thought of corruption, of which it is commonly used as a symbol. (*Cp.* Matt. 16:6 *seq.*, and contrast Matt. 13:33)

to your families, and kill the passover. 22. And ye shall take a bunch of hyssop, and dip it in the blood that is in the basin, and strike the lintel and the two side posts with the blood that is in the basin; and none of you shall go out at the door of his house until the morning. 23. For the Lord will pass through to smite the Egyptians; and when he seeth the blood upon the lintel, and on the two side posts, the Lord will pass over the door, and will not suffer the destroyer to come in unto your houses to smite you. 24. And ye shall observe this thing for an ordinance to thee and to thy sons for ever. 25. And it shall come to pass, when ye be come to the land which the Lord will give you, according as he hath promised, that ye shall keep this service. 26. And it shall come to pass, when your children shall say unto you, What mean ye by this service? 27. that ye shall say, It is the sacrifice of the Lord's passover, who passed over the houses of the children of Israel in Egypt, when he smote the Egyptians, and delivered our houses. And the people bowed the head and worshipped. 28. And the children of Israel went away, and did as the Lord had commanded Moses and Aaron, so did they.

(10b) *Death of the Firstborn* (see chap, 11, p. 172)— 29. And it came to pass, that at midnight the Lord smote all the firstborn in the land of Egypt, from the firstborn of Pharaoh that sat on his throne unto the firstborn of the captive that was in the dungeon; and all the firstborn of cattle. 30. And Pharaoh rose up in the night, he, and all his servants, and all the Egyptians; and there was

22. **hyssop** = marjoram (*Origanum syriacum*): "It grows between stones of ruined wall, and is sold in bunches for sprinkling purposes." (*Murray's Ill*. B.D.)

a great cry in Egypt; for there was not a house where there was not one dead.

Preparations for the Exodus—31. And he called for Moses and Aaron by night, and said, Rise up, and get you forth from among my people, both ye and the children of Israel; and go, serve the Lord, as ye have said. 32. Also take your flocks and your herds, as ye have said, and be gone; and bless me also. 33. And the Egyptians were urgent upon the people, that they might send them out of the land in haste; for they said, We be all dead men. 34. And the people took their dough before it was leavened, their kneadingtroughs being bound up in their clothes upon their shoulders. 35. And the children of Israel did according to the word of Moses; and they borrowed of the Egyptians jewels of silver, and jewels of gold, and raiment: 36. and the Lord gave the people favor in the sight of the Egyptians, so that they lent unto them such things as they required. And they spoiled the Egyptians.

The Exodus—37. And the children of Israel journeyed from Rameses to Succoth, about six hundred thousand on foot that were men, beside children. 38. And a mixed multitude went up also with them; and flocks, and herds, even very much cattle. 39. And they baked unleavened cakes of the dough which they brought forth out of Egypt, for it was not leavened; because they were thrust out

37. Six hundred thousand is an almost impossible number; in 37:26 the number given is even larger; and it does not include women and children. They are supposed to have descended from 70 persons (1:5), who entered Goshen 430 years before. After all, it would be unreasonable to expect statistical accuracy in these early records, edited and compiled, so long after the events described, by men who had a natural tendency to magnify the achievements of the past.

of Egypt, and could not tarry, neither had they prepared for themselves any victual.

40. Now the sojourning of the children of Israel, who dwelt in Egypt, was four hundred and thirty years. 41. And it came to pass at the end of the four hundred and thirty years, even the selfsame day it came to pass, that all the hosts of the Lord went out from the land of Egypt. 42. It is a night to be much observed unto the Lord for bringing them out from the land of Egypt: this is that night of the Lord to be observed of all the children of Israel in their generations.

The Passover and "strangers"—43. And the Lord said unto Moses and Aaron, This is the ordinance of the passover: There shall no stranger eat thereof: 44. but every man's servant that is bought for money, when thou hast circumcised him, then shall he eat thereof. 45. A foreigner and an hired servant shall not eat thereof. 46. In one house shall it be eaten; thou shalt not carry forth ought of the flesh abroad out of the house; neither shall ye break a bone thereof. 47. All the congregation of Israel shall keep it. 48. And when a stranger shall sojourn with thee, and will keep the passover to the Lord, let all his males be circumcised, and then let him come near and keep it; and he shall be as one that is born in the land: for no uncircumcised person shall eat thereof. 49. One law shall be to him that is homeborn, and unto the stranger that sojourneth among you. 50. Thus did all the children of Israel; as the Lord commanded Moses and Aaron, so did they. 51. And it came to pass the

46. **break a bone**. *Cp*. John 19:36.

48. **come near**. vv. 43-50 are from the Priestly source: and this expression probably means "come to the Temple."

selfsame day, that the Lord did bring the children of Israel out of the land of Egypt by their armies.

The importance of the sanctification of the Firstborn—13:1. And the Lord spake unto Moses, saying, 2. Sanctify unto me all the firstborn, whatsoever openeth the womb among the children of Israel, both of man and of beast: it is mine.

3. And Moses said unto the people, Remember this day, in which ye came out from Egypt, out of the house of bondage; for by strength of hand the Lord brought you out from this place: there shall no leavened bread be eaten. 4. This day came ye out in the month Abib. 5. And it shall be when the Lord shall bring thee into the land of the Canaanites, and the Hittites, and the Amorites, and the Hivites, and the Jebusites, which he sware unto thy fathers to give thee, a land flowing with milk and honey, that thou shalt keep this service in this month. 6. Seven days thou shalt eat unleavened bread, and in the seventh day shall be a feast to the Lord. 7. Unleavened bread shall be eaten seven days; and there shall no leavened bread be seen with thee, neither shall there be leaven seen with thee in all thy quarters.

8. And thou shalt shew thy son in that day, saying, This is done because of that which the Lord did unto me when I came forth out of Egypt. 9. And it shall be for a sign unto thee upon thine hand, and for a memorial between thine eyes, that the Lord's law may be in thy mouth: for with a strong hand hath the Lord brought thee out of Egypt. 10. Thou shalt therefore keep this ordinance in his season from year to year. 11. And it shall be when the Lord shall bring thee into the

9. For an explanation of this verse, see on verse 16.

land of the Canaanites, as he sware unto thee and to thy fathers, and shall give it thee, 12. that thou shalt set apart unto the Lord all that openeth the womb, and every firstling that cometh of a beast which thou hast; the males shall be the Lord's. 13. And every firstling of an ass thou shalt redeem with a lamb; and if thou wilt not redeem it, then thou shalt break his neck: and all the firstborn of man among thy children shalt thou redeem.

14. And it shall be when thy son asketh thee in time to come, saying, What is this? that thou shalt say unto him, By strength of hand the Lord brought us out from Egypt, from the house of bondage: 15. and it came to pass, when Pharaoh would hardly let us go, that the Lord slew all the firstborn in the land of Egypt, both the firstborn of man, and the firstborn of beast: therefore I sacrifice to the Lord all that openeth the womb, being males; but all the firstborn of my children I redeem. 16. And it shall be for a token upon thine hand, and for frontlets between thine eyes: for by strength of hand the Lord brought us forth out of Egypt.

The route chosen: and the presence of Jehovah—17. And it came to pass, when Pharaoh had let the people go, that God led them not through the way of the land of the Philistines, although that was near; for God said, Lest

13. **redeem**, *i.e.* buy back (so to speak) from Jehovah by the sacrifice of an inferior creature: otherwise it was to be considered devoted, and so had to be destroyed.

16. **frontlets**. The language here seems to be metaphorical: "it will be a reminder to you"; but parallel passages in Deuteronomy were taken literally, and the Jews wore phylacteries, or frontlets, on the left arm and the forehead: these frontlets were leather boxes containing pieces of parchment on which were written the special passages, *e.g.* Ex. 13:1-10.

17. **Philistines**, *i.e.* by the quickest route to Palestine, due northeast, to the land occupied by the Philistines soon after the Exodus. See on Gen. 21:32.

peradventure the people repent when they see war, and they return to Egypt: 18. but God led the people about, through the way of the wilderness of the Red sea: and the children of Israel went up harnessed out of the land of Egypt. 19. And Moses took the bones of Joseph with him: for he had straitly sworn the children of Israel, saying, God will surely visit you; and ye shall carry up my bones away hence with you.

20. And they took their journey from Succoth, and encamped in Etham, in the edge of the wilderness. 21. And the Lord went before them by day in a pillar of a cloud, to lead them the way; and by night in a pillar of fire, to give them light; to go by day and night: 22. he took not away the pillar of the cloud by day, nor the pillar of fire by night, from before the people.

The pursuit by Pharaoh—14:1. And the Lord spake unto Moses, saying, 2. Speak unto the children of Israel, that they turn and encamp before Pi-hahiroth, between Migdol and the sea, over against Baal-zephon: before it shall ye encamp by the sea. 3. For Pharaoh will say of the children of Israel, They are entangled in the land, the wilderness hath shut them in. 4. And I will harden Pharaoh's heart, that he shall follow after them; and I will be honoured upon Pharaoh, and upon all his host; that the Egyptians may know that I am the Lord. And they did so.

5. And it was told the king of Egypt that the people fled: and the heart of Pharaoh and of his servants was turned against the people, and they said, Why have we done this, that we have let Israel go from serving us? 6. And he made ready his chariot, and took his people with him: 7. and he took six hundred chosen chariots, and

all the chariots of Egypt, and captains over every one of them. 8. And the Lord hardened the heart of Pharaoh king of Egypt, and he pursued after the children of Israel: and the children of Israel went out with an high hand. 9. But the Egyptians pursued after them, all the horses and chariots of Pharaoh, and his horsemen, and his army, and overtook them encamping by the sea, beside Pi-hahiroth, before Baal-zephon.

Murmurings of the Israelites—10. And when Pharaoh drew nigh, the children of Israel lifted up their eyes, and, behold, the Egyptians marched after them; and they were sore afraid: and the children of Israel cried out unto the Lord. ii. And they said unto Moses, Because there were no graves in Egypt, hast thou taken us away to die in the wilderness? wherefore hast thou dealt thus with us, to carry us forth out of Egypt? 12. Is not this the word that we did tell thee in Egypt, saying, Let us alone, that we may serve the Egyptians? For it had been better for us to serve the Egyptians, than that we should die in the wilderness.

13. And Moses said unto the people, Fear ye not, stand still, and see the salvation of the Lord, which he will shew to you to day: for the Egyptians whom ye have seen to day, ye shall see them again no more for ever. 14. The Lord shall fight for you, and ye shall hold your peace.

THE CROSSING OF THE RED SEA

The sites of the three places, Pi-hahiroth, Migdol, and Baal-zephon, are unknown. The Israelites started from

8. **with an high hand** may mean either (1) proudly, or (2) through the act of Jehovah.

Raamses, and reached Succoth, identified with Pithom (Pi-Tum), the position of which we know. The exact spot at which the crossing took place is impossible to decide. The chief alternatives are the northernmost point of the Gulf of Suez, and the southernmost point of the Bitter Lakes east of Goshen. The deliverance of Israel was effected by the providential occurrence of a wind, described in the narrative as east. If the route chosen was across the head of the lake it must have been an exceptionally strong south-east wind, the Sirocco, which would drive the waters of the lake towards the north-west, and allow the Israelites to march safely across. Then, when the wind changed to the north-west, the waters would return at a great speed and overwhelm the pursuing army.

14:15. And the Lord said unto Moses, Wherefore criest thou unto me? speak unto the children of Israel, that they go forward: 16. but lift thou up thy rod, and stretch out thine hand over the sea, and divide it: and the children of Israel shall go on dry ground through the midst of the sea. 17. And I, behold, I will harden the hearts of the Egyptians, and they shall follow them: and I will get me honor upon Pharaoh, and upon all his host, upon his chariots, and upon his horsemen. 18. And the Egyptians shall know that I am the Lord, when I have gotten me honor upon Pharaoh, upon his chariots, and upon his horsemen.

The crossing of the Red Sea, and destruction of the Egyptian army—19. And the angel of God, which went before the camp of Israel, removed and went behind them; and the pillar of the cloud went from before their face, and stood behind them: 20. and it came between the camp of the

Egyptians and the camp of Israel; and it was a cloud and darkness to them, but it gave light by night to these: so that the one came not near the other all the night. 21. And Moses stretched out his hand over the sea; and the Lord caused the sea to go back by a strong east wind all that night, and made the sea dry land, and the waters were divided. 22. And the children of Israel went into the midst of the sea upon the dry ground: and the waters were a wall unto them on their right hand, and on their left. 23. And the Egyptians pursued, and went in after them to the midst of the sea, even all Pharaoh's horses, his chariots, and his horsemen. 24. And it came to pass, that in the morning watch the Lord looked unto the host of the Egyptians through the pillar of fire and of the cloud, and troubled the host of the Egyptians, 25. and took off their chariot wheels, that they drave them heavily: so that the Egyptians said, Let us flee from the face of Israel; for the Lord fighteth for them against the Egyptians. 26. And the Lord said unto Moses, Stretch out thine hand over the sea, that the waters may come again upon the Egyptians, upon their chariots, and upon their horsemen. 27. And Moses stretched forth his hand over the sea, and the sea returned to his strength when the morning appeared; and the Egyptians fled against it; and the Lord overthrew the Egyptians in the midst of the sea. 28. And the waters returned, and covered the chariots,

20. **and it was a cloud... to these**. R.V. "and there was the cloud and the darkness, yet gave it light by night." The A.V. represents an attempt to make sense of a difficult passage, of which no certain solution has been found.

24. **morning watch**. The night, from sunset to sunrise, was divided into three equal watches: the Romans divided it into four. Both systems were used by Jews in N.T. times.

25. **took off**. R.V. marg., "Some ancient versions read, *bound*." This gives a more natural sense, referring to the heavy ground.

and the horsemen, and all the host of Pharaoh that came into the sea after them; there remained not so much as one of them. 29. But the children of Israel walked upon dry land in the midst of the sea; and the waters were a wall unto them on their right hand, and on their left. 30. Thus the Lord saved Israel that day out of the hand of the Egyptians; and Israel saw the Egyptians dead upon the sea shore. 31. And Israel saw that great work which the Lord did upon the Egyptians: and the people feared the Lord, and believed the Lord, and his servant Moses.

The song of Moses—15:1. Then sang Moses and the children of Israel this song unto the Lord, and spake, saying,

I will sing unto the Lord, for he hath triumphed gloriously: the horse and his rider hath he thrown into the sea.

2. The Lord is my strength and song, and he is become my salvation: he is my God, and I will prepare him an habitation; my father's God, and I will exalt him.

3. The Lord is a man of war: the Lord is his name.

4. Pharaoh's chariots and his host hath he cast into the sea: his chosen captains also are drowned in the Red Sea.

1. **rider**, *i.e.* charioteer.

1-18. "In beauty of style, forceful and nervous language, and poetic skill, this song is unsurpassed. It stands as one of the finest specimens of Hebrew lyric poetry" (McNeile, *Exodus*, p. 88). The principal differences in the R.V. are as follows:

A.V.	R.V.
2. prepare him an habitation.	praise him.
14. The people shall hear, and be afraid: sorrow shall take hold on the inhabitants of Palestina.	The peoples have heard, they tremble: pangs have taken hold on the inhabitants of Philistia.
15. shall be . . . shall take hold . . . shall melt.	were . . . taketh hold . . . are melted.
16. shall fall . . . shall be.	falleth . . . they are.

5. The depths have covered them: they sank into the bottom as a stone.

6. Thy right hand, O Lord, is become glorious in power: thy right hand, O Lord, hath dashed in pieces the enemy.

7. And in the greatness of thine excellency thou hast overthrown them that rose up against thee: thou sentest forth thy wrath, which consumed them as stubble.

8. And with the blast of thy nostrils the waters were gathered together, the floods stood upright as an heap, and the depths were congealed in the heart of the sea.

9. The enemy said, I will pursue, I will overtake, I will divide the spoil; my lust shall be satisfied upon them; I will draw my sword, my hand shall destroy them.

10. Thou didst blow with thy wind, the sea covered them: they sank as lead in the mighty waters.

11. Who is like unto thee, O Lord, among the gods? who is like thee, glorious in holiness, fearful in praises, doing wonders?

12. Thou stretchedst out thy right hand, the earth swallowed them.

13. Thou in thy mercy hast led forth the people which thou hast redeemed: thou hast guided them in thy strength unto thy holy habitation.

14. The people shall hear, and be afraid: sorrow shall take hold on the inhabitants of Palestina.

15. Then the dukes of Edom shall be amazed; the

13-18. This song is almost certainly of later date than Moses: his is shown most clearly in these verses, which imply a knowledge of the entrance into Canaan and the centralization of national worship at Jerusalem.

15. **dukes** = chieftains.

mighty men of Moab, trembling shall take hold upon them; all the inhabitants of Canaan shall melt away.

16. Fear and dread shall fall upon them; by the greatness of thine arm they shall be as still as a stone; till thy people pass over, O Lord, till the people pass over, which thou hast purchased.

17. Thou shalt bring them in, and plant them in the mountain of thine inheritance, in the place, O Lord, which thou hast made for thee to dwell in, in the Sanctuary, O Lord, which thy hands have established.

18. The Lord shall reign for ever and ever.

19. For the horse of Pharaoh went in with his chariots and with his horsemen into the sea, and the Lord brought again the waters of the sea upon them; but the children of Israel went on dry land in the midst of the sea.

The song of Miriam—20. And Miriam the prophetess, the sister of Aaron, took a timbrel in her hand; and all the women went out after her with timbrels and with dances. 21. And Miriam answered them, Sing ye to the Lord, for he hath triumphed gloriously; the horse and his rider hath he thrown into the sea.

18. The song of Moses ends with this verse: verse 19 is a compiler's "gloss," summarizing the historical facts.

19. **horse**. Read "horses."

Pharaoh. It is not stated, either here or in 14:28, that Pharaoh himself was drowned. The mummy of Merenptah has been identified with practical certainty. However, both here and in Psalm 136:5, the death of Pharaoh is distinctly implied; and it must be remembered that there is no absolute proof of the identification of Merenptah with the Pharaoh of the Exodus.

20. **the prophetess**. The title here, as in the case of Deborah, signifies poetic inspiration. Probably the "song of Miriam" is simply the Elohistic version of the "Song of Moses," which belongs to the Jehovistic source.

APPENDIXES

APPENDIX I

THE FORMATION OF THE OLD TESTAMENT

CANON

1. Canon primarily means the "standard" to which a book, or portion of a book, must attain in respect of its historical, moral, and religious value, in order to be ranked among the authoritative sacred Scriptures. Hence the term, from being used of the standard by which a book was judged, has come to be applied to the body of books themselves, which have satisfied the requirements of this standard. Thus the "Old Testament Canon" means those sacred books of Hebrew literature which were judge by the Hebrews to satisfy these requirements, just as the "New Testament Canon" means that body of sacred books which were judged by the early Christian Church to satisfy the requirements of the Christian standard. These two bodies of sacred literature, the one translated from the original Hebrew and Aramaic, the other translated from the original Greek, together form our Bible.

Besides those books which are included in the Old Testament and the New Testament, there existed many, and exist some, which, though valuable in their religious and moral teaching, were yet not considered sufficiently valuable to be admitted respectively into the Old Testament and New Testament Canons. Such books are called

Apocryphal; that is, obscure, unrecognized, or spurious. Some of these are comprised in the "Apocrypha," which is often bound up with our modern Bibles, being placed after the end of the Old Testament. Parts of this are read in the English Church services, since they afford a good "example of life and instruction of manners." There is, derived from the other two, yet a third meaning of the term "Canon." Since the sacred writings which are admitted into the Bible conform to a given standard, so in their turn they form the standard by which religious doctrines are judged. A doctrine, or belief, is canonical if it can be justified by the authority of the. canonical books of the Bible; it is uncanonical, though not necessarily wrong, if it cannot thus be proved.

2. How and when was it decided which of the books of Hebrew sacred literature were worthy to be accounted canonical, and which should be relegated to the lower sphere of uncanonical works? In other words, when did the Hebrews decide what was, and what was not, part of their "Bible"? The answer is this. The Canon was not suddenly fixed by any one body of men, by any council, nor at any one time. It was the gradual result of criticism, appreciation, use, and experience. If any part of their sacred writings was felt by the Jews to be valuable and useful and helpful and true, and was therefore continuously used by them as a source of their knowledge of God, and recognized as being part of His message by which He gradually, and more and more clearly as time went on, revealed Himself to them and showed them what He would have them be, and what His purpose was towards them, then this part would be accepted by them as authoritative or canonical. Thus *part* of the

Canon would have become fixed. Later on, another part would, by a similar critical process, be added to their Canon; and eventually, by about the time of our Lord, the entire Canon of the Old Testament, as we have it, would have been completed. We can, as a matter of fact, trace, though not with perfect clearness, this process. In quite early days the Decalogue was accepted in this way. It had been delivered to the Israelites by Moses, of whose personality only the most extreme critics of the Bible have ever had any doubt. To this were added in course of time the other different and more highly developed injunctions of the Hebrew law; until, after the specific promulgation of the Deuteronomic law by

King Josiah in 621 B.C., and the careful collection of all their legislative documents by the scholars of the Exile, the first great part of the Canon, the Law (Torah), which we call the Pentateuch, was completed (445 B.C.).

By degrees, and by the same tests—the value, truth, and inspiration of the books—there was added to the Canon its second great volume, the Prophets (Nebhiim), as the Jews called it. This volume consisted of the following books: Joshua, Judges, Samuel, Kings, Isaiah, Jeremiah, Ezekiel, and the Twelve Minor Prophets, from Hosea to Malachi. This part of the Canon was defined before the end of the third century B.C.

The third volume of the Canon, which was called the Sacred Writings (Kethubhim, or in Greek, Hagiographa), embraced the Psalms, the Song of Solomon, Lamentations, Ruth, Chronicles, Ezra, Nehemiah, Esther, the prophet Daniel, and the Sapiential Literature, *i.e.* Proverbs, Job, and Ecclesiastes. It was probably accepted into the Canon by about the Christian era, though the date is not

I—13

certain. Daniel, which was the last book of the Old Testament to be composed (165 B.C.), is quoted by our Lord, who refers by name, too, to the other two volumes, the Law and the Prophets; but some books in this last volume are not mentioned by our Lord or the apostles, and it is therefore argued by some that this volume was not entirely complete in their day. But this negative argument from silence is not conclusive evidence; and it is certain that the Jewish Bible in our Lord's time was practically, if not completely, identical with the Old Testament Canon as we have it. Thus the Old Testament Canon rests upon the highest possible authority, no less than that of Christ Himself. [1]

3. A word remains to be said upon the earliest version of the Hebrew Bible in a foreign language—that called the Septuagint, in Greek. This translation was rendered necessary owing to the spread of the Greek tongue as a familiar vehicle of speech, side by side with the vernacular Aramaic, throughout Syria and Palestine in the third and second centuries before Christ. Tradition has it that the work of translation was begun in the third century B.C., at Alexandria, under the auspices of Ptolemy Philadelphus, King of Egypt from 285 to 247 B.C. Of this we cannot be certain. But it is known with certainty that the work was only achieved slowly. The "Law "was the first part to be translated, and then the work was continued at different times and by different hands. Some portions of the version are far inferior to others, both in accuracy and style. At some date before the end of the pre-Christian era the translation of the whole Canon was

[1]See G. Adam Smith, *Modern Criticism and the Preaching of the Old Testament*, Lecture I.

eventually completed; and the result was, and is, most valuable as an assistance to the correction and interpretation of the Hebrew text as it has come down to us.

APPENDIX II

SOME REFERENCES TO CONTEMPORARY MESOPOTAMIAN AND EGYPTIAN HISTORY AND TRADITIONS

To the date of the Crossing of the Red Sea

References—"D.G." are to pages in *Genesis*, Driver
(Westminster Commentaries).
" "B. L. E." are to pages in *Light from the East*, Ball.
" "McNeile" *Exodus*, McNeile (Westminster
Commentaries).

I. MESOPOTAMIA

1. *Creation Narratives*.
D. G. 26-31 and 51-4.
For the second Bible narrative, see also B. L. E.
18-21.
2. *Paradise* ("Edinu," Sacred Tree and Cherubim)
D.G. 51-4; B.L.E. 28-33.
3. *"Adam"*
D.G. note on Gen. 2, verse 20. B.L.E. 20-21.
4. *Flood Narratives*.
D.G. 80, 103-8.
5. *Nimrod* (Gen. x. 8-12).
D.G. 122-3.
6. *Tower of Babel*.
D.G. 136-7. B.L.E. 69.

7. *Ur of the Chaldees.*

        D.G. 48, 49, 142 footnote.

8. *Amraphel* (— Hammurabi), etc., Gen. 14.

        D.G. 156-8, 171-3. B.L.E. 65-70. McNeile
        39, 47 seq.

II. Egypt

XVth—XVIIth Dynasties (*Hyksos Kings*).

        D. G. 347.

        McNeile 12.

        D.G. 346 (Baba).

XVIIIth Dynasty (*Thothmes* III.).

        D.G. 51, 52 (name Yacob-el in Palestine).

Amenhotep III and IV. (Tel-el-Amarna Letters).

        D.G. 29, 125, 167-8.

        B.L.E. 86-94.

XIXth Dynasty (*Ramses II*).

        McNeile. Addenda (Raamses).

        McNeile. 93, 94. (Pithom).

        B.L.E. 109-13 (Slave-labor in Egypt).

        D.G. 52. (Mt. of Asher).

Merenptah.

        McNeile 13 (The Pharaoh of the Exodus).

        McNeile. 109 and note, and B.L.E. 129 (" Israel
        is desolated").

        McNeile. 110 and note (Frontier Policy).

        N.B.—See also *Authority and Archeology*, ed. by D. G. Hogarth, Part First.

APPENDIX III

References to *Bible Illustrations,* Appendix to *"Helps to the Study of the Bible"*: Oxford University Press, 1896.

Plate 55 . . .   Ra, the Sun-god.
"   58 . . .   Embalming in Egypt.
"   59. . . .   Ramses II.
"   67-69 . . . Ramses II.
"   70 . . .   Strangers coming into Egypt.
"   71 . . .   Egyptian granaries.
"   72, 73. . . Brick-making in Egypt.

APPENDIX IV

SOME NEW TESTAMENT REFERENCES

Gen. 1:27_
       | Creation of man and woman.   Matt. 19:3-6
  2:24_|
  2:2 The Sabbath rest   Heb. 4:4
  2:7 The first man, Adam   1 Cor. 15:45
      Summary of history from time
      of Abraham. . .   Acts 7
  22:18 | The blessing on the seed of   Acts 3:25
  12:3 | Abraham   Gal. 3:8
      The faith of Abraham . . .   Rom. 4
      Abel, Enoch, Noah, Abraham,
      Isaac, Jacob, Joseph, and
      Moses, as examples of faith,   Heb. 11
21:1-21 Children of promise, as
      opposed to children of
      bondage . . . .   Gal. 4:21-5:1

Ex. 3:6	The God of the living . . .	Matt. 12:32
9:16	God's divine purpose . . .	Rom. 9:17
12:46	"A bone of him shall not be broken	John 19:36.
13:2	The sanctification of the firstborn	Luke 2:23

APPENDIX V

THE CALENDAR OF THE JEWISH YEAR

ORDER IN THE		MONTH	ENGLISH EQUIVALENT, APPROXIMATELY
CIVIL YEAR*	SACRED YEAR*		
7	i.	Nisan or Abib.	April
8	ii.	Ziv or Xyyar.	May
9	iii.	Sivan	June
10	iv.	Tammuz.	July
11	v.	Ab.	August
12	vi.	Elul.	September
1	vii.	Tishri or Ethanim.	October
2	viii.	Marcheshvan or Bui	November
3	ix.	Chisleu.	December
4	x.	Tebeth.	January
5	xi.	Shebat.	February
6	xii.	Adar.	March

* The "civil" year is the older Hebrew year, which began in autumn. But in early days, before the Exile, the Babylonian calendar, by which the year began in spring, was also in use in Palestine. This latter calendar was adopted for ritual purposes, and the festivals were arranged according to it. Therefore, the year according to this computation is called the "sacred" year.

Akaba, half-way between Beer-sheba and Elath

Kadmonites (Gen. 15:19), a tribe E. of Canaan.

Kenites (Gen. 15:19), a tribe in S. Ca naan.

Kenizzites (Gen. 15:19), a tribe in S. Canaan.

Kirfath-arba (Gen. 23:2) — Hebron.

Lahai-roi (Gen. 24:62, 25:11) = Beer-lahai-roi.

Luz (Gen. 28:19, 35:6) = Beth-el.

Machpelah, cave of (Gen. 23:9, 25:9, 50:13), near Hebron.

Mahanaim (Gen. 32:2), in Gilead, near R. Jordan.

Mamre (Gen. 23:17) — Hebron.

Mesopotamia (Gen. 24:10), country be tween R. Tigris and R. Euphrates.

Midian (Ex. 2:15 seq.), S.E. of Canaan, E. of G. of Akaba.

Midianites (Gen. 37:28), people of Midian.

Migdol (Ex. 14:2), somewhere E. of Delta of R. Nile.

Mizpah (Gen. 31:49), a height in Gil ead.

Mizraim (Gen. 10:6) Egypt.

Moriah, Land of (Gen. 12:2), unknown.

Nineveh (Gen. 10:11), capital of Assyr ia, on R. Tigris.

Nod (Gen. 4:16), unknown; 'east of Eden.'

On (Gen. 41:45) = Heliopolis, N.E. of Cairo.

Pad an-ar am (Gen. 25:20, 28:2 seq.), district round Haran, in Mesopotamia.

Paran, Wilderness of (Gen. 21:21), due N. of G. of Akaba.

Peniel, Penuel (Gen. 32:30, 31), E. of Jordan, S. of R. Jabbok.

Perizzites (Gen. 13:7, 15:20, Ex. 3:8), a Canaanite tribe.

Philistines (Gen. 21:32, 26:1), S.W. of Palestine, W. of Judah.

Pi-hahiroth (Ex. 14:2, 9), somewhere to N.W. of Suez.

Pison (Gen. 2:11), unknown; a river of Eden.

Pithom (Ex. 1:11), practically identi cal with Succoth; due W. of the Bitter Lakes, N.W. of G. of Suez.

Raamses (Ex. 1:11), 8 m. S.W. of Pithom, E. of the Nile Delta.

Rameses (Ex. 12:37) = Raamses.

Rameses, Land of (Gene. 47:11), district E. of Nile Delta.

Rephaims (Gen. 14:5, 15:20), a giant people of S.W. Canaan.

Salem (Gen. 14:18) = Jerusalem.

Seir (Gen. 14:6, 32:3, 33:14 seq.), coun try of the Edomites, S.E. of Palestine.

Shalem (Gen. 33:18), close to Shechem.

Shaveh, Valley of (Gen. 14:17), near Je rusalem.

Shaveh Kiviathaim (Gen. 14:5), N. of R. Arnon, E. of Dead Sea.

Shechem (Gen. 33:18, 35:4,37:12-14), centre of hill country E. of Plain of Sharon, between Mts. Ebal and Gerizim.

Shinar (Gen. 10:10, 11:2) = Babylonia.

Shur (Gen. 16:7, 20:1, 25:18), district beyond the E. borders of Egypt.

Sichem (Gen. 12: 6) = Shechem.

Siddim, Vale of (Gen. 14:3, 10), S. of Dead Sea.

Sodom (Gen. 13:10 seq., 14:2, 18:20 seq.), S. of Dead Sea.

Succoth (1) (Gen. 33:17), E. of R. Jordan, near R. Jabbok.
(2) (Ex. 12:37, 13:20) = Pi-thom, in Egypt.

Ur of the Chaldees (Gen. 11:28), half-way between Babylon and Persian Gulf.

Zeboiim (Gen. 14:2), S. of Dead Sea.
Zoav (Gen. 13:10, 19:22), S. of Dead Sea.
Zuzims (Gen. 14:5), giant people N.E. of Dead Sea.

GENERAL   INDEX

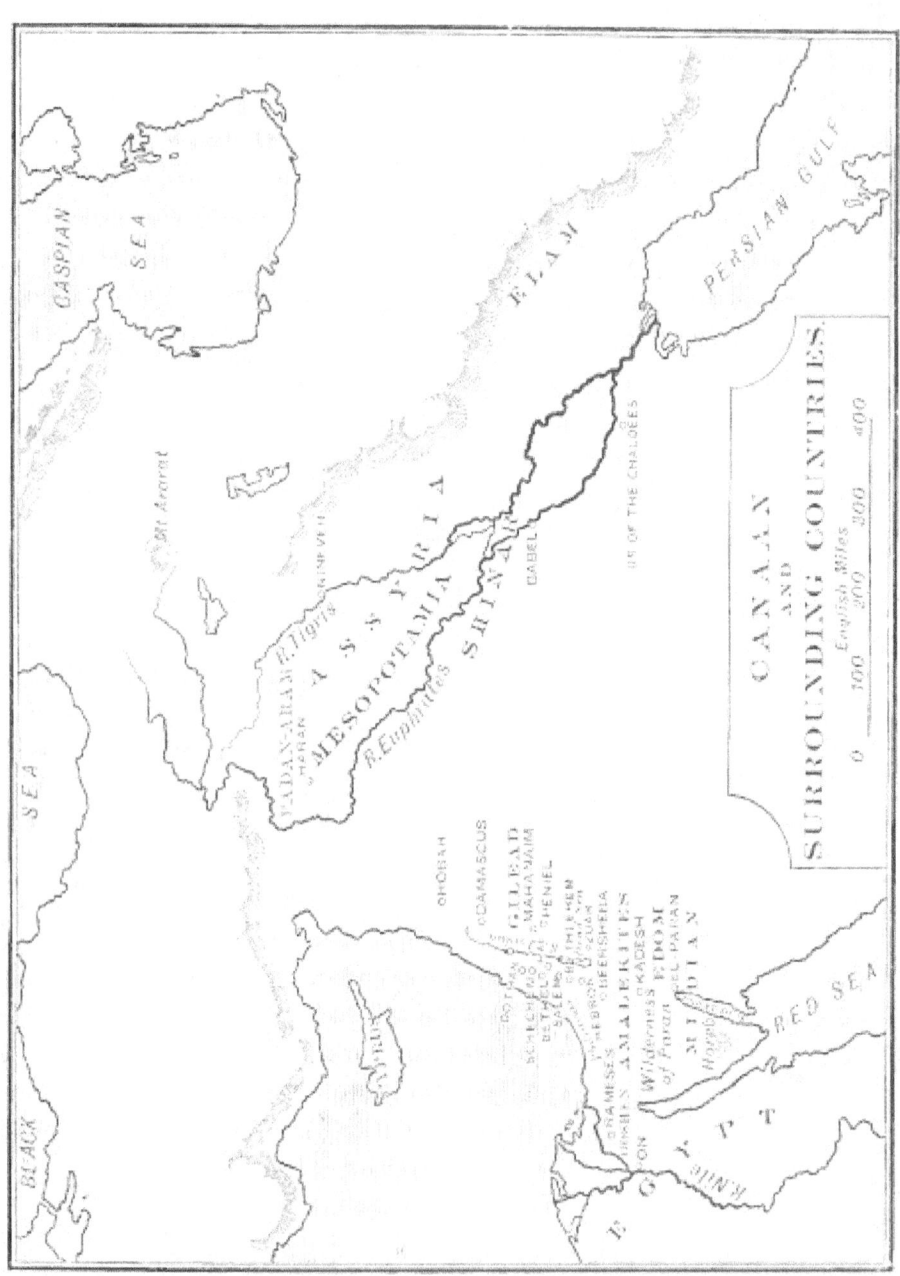

208